EMPOV
BY
STY

DRESS FOR YOUR PERSONALITY
LOOK GREAT AND FEEL CONFIDENT EVERY DAY

MARY GRANT

Published by Known Publishing, 2020.

ISBN 978-1-913036-32-4

KNOWN

www.get-known.co.uk

Dedication

To all my wonderful customers who supported every collection over the years. We have laughed and cried together. We have kept eachother going through life's ups and downs from raising kids to illnesses, divorces, second marriages and loss. This is for you.

Testimonials

"I looked at my reflection in the mirror and tears spilled down my face. I then looked at my mum and sister, there were tears in their eyes too.

You see, six months earlier I had had a double mastectomy and was finding it very difficult to get used to my new shape. We were going to a family wedding and nothing I put on worked! I found it very difficult to find clothes that made me feel feminine and not like a square, which is what my new shape was. When I looked at my reflection that day I felt like me again, the me before any illness, the confident me.

I have been buying Mary's clothes for the last 25 years. Every time I put a piece on, I feel I am putting a new brick in my confidence wall. When you wear Mary's collections, you feel like each piece has been made specially for you"

-SYLVIA MCHENRY-

"I discovered Mary Grant in London, over 20 years ago. I loved strutting around in my big boots and black patch pocket dungarees and being stopped in the street and asked where they came from. Without following trends, Mary has found a unique and timeless style that remarkably suits women of all ages. Each piece mixes and matches with previous collections to encompass urban chic, classic, modern, romantic or just a cosy comfortable style. How she does it, I do not know, I'm just grateful she does.

Twenty years on and advancing years bring many mixed feelings and insecurities. Mary's timeless designs help to restore a belief that it's OK to feel good about yourself; you are important and you can and should be able to look and feel good at any age. I love that I can still buy and wear her clothes, dress them up with a beautiful jacket, cashmere wrap or funky jewellery, or just wear them casually around the house being a "cool mum"!

-MICHAELA TARLTON-

"Not so long ago, I discovered I had a thyroid problem which affected my weight. When you go up 3 dress sizes in as many months, it's all you can think about. I didn't like what I saw in the mirror and I didn't know my shape. I was lost.

I thought that I would never look or feel as confident as I used to before the thyroid condition hit me.

With a special occasion coming up, I was getting very stressed out and finding myself in one of Mary's stores, I finally spilled it all out to the wonderful stylist who helped me to rediscover the old me and dress for my new shape.

I don't know if I looked pretty but what mattered was that I felt beautiful."

-SIOBHAN CONWAY-

"I travel a lot and need a versatile easy care wardrobe that doesn't wrinkle. As I was approaching a big birthday, I was wandering around Dublin looking for inspiration. I stumbled across the Mary Grant store where the wonderful stylists showed me how the collection could be mixed and matched. I left with pieces that made me feel great

for my special birthday and which travel really well and take up very little space in my suitcase. I am complimented everywhere I go when I am wearing them."

-EILEEN MCNALLY-

"I used to think that I needed to be going somewhere special to get dressed up but now I do it every day because it makes me feel so confident and stylish. I have built my mix and match MG collection over many years with pieces that are seasonless and I can dress up everyday pieces for more special occasions."

-CATHERINE TUOHY-

"Down through the years, I have been inspired by Mary Grant's collections. I have enjoyed wearing her timeless winter and summer pieces and rely on her wonderful basics to build my wardrobe. They give me confidence by camouflaging my not so great bits and help me to enhance the better parts of me."

-MARGUERITE GORDAN-

"I needed a special outfit for my daughter's wedding. Being a regular customer, I knew the Mary Grant team would look after me. The outfit was flattering, stylish and suited to the occasion. I got so many compliments and I could wear the pieces separately afterwards. Thank you for making me shop wisely and carefully."

-ROISIN O'CONNOR HANNIGAN-

"I suffer from GAD (General Anxiety Disorder). I have been a worrier as long as I can remember.

I guess we all have that critical voice in our head, saying we're too old or too fat or too wrinkly to wear something. The day Mary invited me to take part on a fun photoshoot, that critical voice was silenced forever. I felt a million dollars. Since then, I have become more experimental with what I wear. Now, instead of being so critical of myself, I am learning to embrace who I am. I'm not perfect. And that's OK. That day had a huge impact on my life!"

-EMMA PEPPARD-

"I first discovered Mary Grant in 2006. I bought a black pinafore and remember her saying that it was a timeless piece and how right she was!

I've bought many more things over the years, but my black pinafore is still my favourite thing.

Even today, every time I wear it, I receive compliments. Thank you, Mary, for your amazing style and for designing for real women."

-SINEAD VAN DER HOEVEN-

Contents

SECTION 7:
TOP TIPS...309

BOOK EXTRAS...357

About This Book

When we are faced with too much choice, we often don't make any. Fashion trends and the range of high street options can be so overwhelming that we end up mindlessly buying clothes that look great on models and influencers, but are not quite right for us.

As with lots of other areas of our lives, we are not taking the time to assess who we are and what works best for us. We end up sleepwalking through life in clothes that say nothing about us, throwing on the nearest thing that comes to hand when we drag ourselves out of bed in the morning. This is uninspiring and does nothing for our confidence or self-esteem.

We are missing a trick. There is another way. In this book, I will show you how to develop and evolve your own personal style. When you do this, you will be free from trends forever. You will be able to see past the racks of choices and zoom in on the pieces that are perfect for you.

You will have your own unique personal style that tells the world exactly who you are.

You will have the power to be whoever you want to be, and that will put you firmly on track to achieving anything you want to achieve. When you go through the process I share in this book, and practice being your true self every day, the results will touch every area of your life. You will be unstoppable.

Who is This Book For?

I have written this book for you if:

- You want to dress for your own personality and ditch fashion trends.
- You want to be the most fabulous version of yourself every day.
- You have a vision for your life that you are trying to achieve.
- You have a hectic life juggling work and/or family and often feel like you meet yourself coming back.
- Life has thrown you a curveball, and your confidence has taken a hit.
- You feel like you are stuck in a rut.
- A big life event is looming and it is proving to be quite stressful.

What you will learn

In section 1, you will become aware of how easy it is to become stuck in a rut whilst juggling a chaotic life and how this affects your self-confidence. You will also learn how to overcome it and prevent it from happening again.

In section 2, we will uncover the buying mistakes that result in so much waste and clutter in your life, and leave you feeling uninspired and unempowered. We will also reveal why what you wear matters, as well as how it affects your mindset and influences your results.

In section 3, we will learn more about you. There is a fun quiz to find out your style archetype. You will learn how to use colour, and you will find out how to dress for your body shape.

In section 4, I will demystify the different wardrobe-building types so that you can decide which best suits your needs and lifestyle.

In section 5, we will do a little bit of mindset work, so that you can develop the confidence to show up as your true self. You will then go on to develop your personal style.

In section 6, we will get physical with your wardrobe and decide what is staying, what is going and what you need to buy. You will also learn the importance of updating your wardrobe as the seasons change.

In section 7, I will share styling, shopping and garment care tips, so that you will spend less and save loads of time for all the other more important things in life.

This book is going to take you on a repeatable journey of assessing your style personality and evolving it, inch by inch, over time. While there is quite a lot of information in this book, it is not a book just to be consumed. Knowing how to do it won't get you the results, so be sure to work through the sections and chapters step by step to get the full value out of it.

In terms of a time commitment, you could work through the whole process in a weekend if you were really motivated and you will certainly get faster each time you do it. However, for the first time, I would prefer you to take your time and do a little bit each evening over a week or two, allowing a weekend for tackling your wardrobe at the end. This is a creative process that you can benefit hugely from when you trust and follow the process. You will benefit from taking breaks as you go along because this is when your thinking evolves.

When you have completed this process, you won't have to think about your wardrobe again for the next six months. You will have a versatile wardrobe that works for you every day and you will have social events and occasions planned for in advance. This will make you more confident and enable you to show up in the world as the best version of yourself. Shopping trips will be more focused and more enjoyable. You will spend less time shopping and be less overwhelmed by choice. You will eliminate buying mistakes, allowing you to spend more on the pieces that you really love, which you can wear every day.

The process can be completed for the first time wherever you are at right now and whatever time of the year it is. You only need to repeat the process twice a year at the turn of the seasons. After that, you will just be adding some high summer and deep winter pieces as top-up basics. You will get faster, your thoughts will become clearer, and you will be more confident in your own style each time you do it.

I have created vision boards to help you become clear on what you love and why. I will walk you through how to create your own vision board, which will inspire and empower you, season after season, year after year.

This book has been edited and re-edited to a point where my brain was on fire. Every chapter that made the cut has earned its place. By the time we have finished, I want you to be the most empowered, confident and inspired version of yourself that you have ever been in your life, so don't be tempted to gloss over sections.

The secret to the biggest outcomes is to learn all the secrets along the way and to do the work ... step by step!

SECTION 1

Evolving Through Life

"If I am not good to myself,
how can I expect anyone else to be good to me?"

MAYA ANGELOU

Introduction to Section 1

In this section, I will show you how easy it is to find yourself stuck in a rut and show you how this can start to affect all areas of your life without you even noticing. I'm also going to share my own personal story of getting myself well and truly stuck. It happens to us all whilst we are busy dealing with everyday life.

This section is all about awareness. I want you to be aware of the problem, how it can hit when you least expect it and how it can take you down, hijacking your confidence for months on end unless you have a strategy in place to prevent it.

I will share the elements of my own journey with you that brought me to a place where I am passionate about making women feel fabulous and confident every day.

Finally, in this section, I want you to be aware of how the power of constantly evolving right through your life ensures that you are relevant and the most confident version of you at every stage because each one will require a different version of you. I also want you to see how a little bit of work twice a year will leave you feeling on top of things every day rather than constantly feeling like you are on the back foot.

CHAPTER 1

Juggler to Superhero

The world is spinning faster and faster. Life has you meeting yourself coming back. Between work and family life, it's a permanent juggling act. You find yourself in a constant chaotic state of physical and mental overwhelm as you duck and dive in an effort to stay on top of it all. On the surface you are a swan gliding down the river, underneath you are paddling like the clappers. You are handling it all, apparently without even breaking into a sweat.

You have little or no time to dedicate to yourself, which takes its toll, until something happens that gets your attention, long enough for you to realise that you are stuck in a rut. You look in the mirror and you are not happy with what you see. This has a detrimental effect on your confidence and self-esteem and leaves you questioning everything.

Everybody around you benefits from hanging out with the happiest and most confident version of you.

You are living your life on default, looking after everybody else's needs and feeling uninspired, unempowered, lacking in direction and downright invisible. Occasionally, you tackle this head-on, like a woman possessed, sending your family fleeing for cover as you try to reclaim a bit of yourself. But this is like putting a Band-Aid on a bullet hole. The time has come for you to get to the root of the problem.

The purpose of this book is to give you a bit of time, space and direction to concentrate on you. I want to help you become strategic in how you show up in your life and be true to yourself. You can make a choice to hold on to a bit of yourself and keep your dreams alive, which inspires everybody around you, including the little people who look up to you.

We are going to spend a bit of time getting to know who you are, what you are trying to get done and how you want to be seen by those around you. You are going to get more clarity on your personal style. You are going to realise why it is so important to take a bit of guilt-free time to reconnect with yourself on an ongoing basis, so that you can be a happier, calmer and more confident version of yourself. You are going to realise how doing the work in this book creates a shift in your mindset that will keep your own dreams alive and open you up to all kinds of opportunities.

Everybody around you benefits from hanging out with the happiest and most confident version of you.

I want you to think about how you feel on those rare occasions when you had plenty of time to get ready. Most likely it was a special occasion like a wedding. You had booked a whole day out from your life, laid out a new outfit that you loved and spent an hour in the hairdressers getting a blow-dry. You took your time doing your makeup and you left the house feeling like a million dollars.

Now, suppose you could have a 5-minute version of that every day which made you feel like you were ready to take on the world. I'm going to show you how to make looking great and feeling confident a habit, so that you are your most confident self every day, even when no one is looking.

CHAPTER 2

25 Years of Observation

I just want to share my background so that you can see how I ended up in this place where I am so passionate about helping women to be the most confident and empowered version of themselves every day.

My body issues

As a teenager, at the age of about 13 or 14, my height shot up to 5' 10" very quickly. I was gangly and awkward. Kids are merciless and name-calling was not frowned upon then the way it is today. I was 'Big Bird', 'Larry the Lamp-post', 'Beanpole' and 'The only girl in Dublin with two backs' (Irish humour which means flat-chested!). I hated attracting attention. It made me want to disappear. If I could go back today, I would tell that teenager a different story and show her how to own it all, but we live and learn! At the time, it was less stressful to just stay out of the spotlight.

I was always at my happiest creating and making. I could lose myself for hours and days on end in my bedroom making clothes, with seams so perfect that you could wear them inside out. By the time I left school, I was making and wearing all my own clothes. I had an obsession with constructing complicated pieces, and to this day, you will often find me staring into space when I'm designing, as I work through the steps of putting a garment together in my head.

My design ethos

After finishing my degree in fashion design, I immediately started my own business. From my own experience with body image issues, I observed that everybody had something about themselves that they didn't love and this, without fail, blinded them to their assets. It became my mission to change how women felt about themselves by designing clothes that allowed them to play down what they don't like without making a big deal of it.

Every season, I would surprise my ever-growing customer base with new designs, perfecting cuts that suited lots of different body shapes. I wasn't so much concerned about turnover and profit as seeing people's faces light up as they walked through the door of my studio on launch day of a new season. Over the years, I noticed that customers' confidence grew in front of my eyes when I pointed out what their assets were. This became my rocket fuel.

Then I started to notice all the places in life where people were getting stuck and that added another new dimension to my work...

CHAPTER 3

Speed Wobbles and Bumpy Roads

Turning 40

I have never been a fan of birthdays, especially the BIG ones. So, as 40 was looming, I was having a bit of a crisis. I had the totally irrational belief that as a designer, I would be over the hill. Even though there was no evidence of this in my physical world and I was enjoying more and more success with every collection I launched, my inner world was having a meltdown. Now that I have hit 50, it seems hilarious when I look back, but at the time 40 was a huge roadblock for me.

Along with all the other nonsense that was going on in my head, I will never forget the day when I stood in my wardrobe and thought, "I hate all this, I have nothing to wear." My wardrobe was full of random pieces from my own collections, a mishmash of colours and styles which I had got loads of wear out of over the years, but I just thought "none of this works for me anymore".

Finding myself newly single in my mid-thirties, with three kids under the age of five, meant that the roundabout which was my life was spinning faster and faster. With everything that being a mum entailed, along with being so busy making everybody else look fabulous, I had been neglecting myself. I was feeling unattractive, uninspired and irrelevant. I hadn't been evolving, I hadn't been keeping in touch with who I was, what I loved, how I wanted to show up. I was living on automatic pilot. I hadn't seen it coming, and I was feeling well and truly stuck! All around me, I noticed the same thing happening to people everywhere, and in the last 10 years I have seen it happen to hundreds of women who are at different stages in their lives. At least several times a week, we will help people to get back on track with cups of tea and a styling session to help them get back in touch with themselves. In the next chapter, I will share all the ways that I have seen people getting stuck.

I have always had a direct-to-consumer business model. It wasn't intentionally planned that way, but even before our own stores, when we were wholesaling and I was running a full-time concession in Brown Thomas for 5 years, I always had a studio in my home, which was open to the public in the afternoons. Both of these allowed me to have a close relationship with my customers and I was often found on the shop floor chatting to them, hearing about their life challenges. These insights and feedback from my team every day helped me to evolve my collections from one season to the next. Even today, when the business has grown to a point where I cannot spend so much time on the shop floor, I eagerly wait for feedback from our stylists at the end of each day.

I hear stories every day about customers who have got stuck in ruts for all kinds of reasons. If we can catch them the first time, we can help them to avoid getting stuck over and over, but for some people, the reality is that they carry on being unaware and every big life event can take them down. As well as big birthdays, other reasons include pregnancies, births, raising families, marriages, divorces, deaths, illnesses, empty nests and retirement. All of these things can throw people into a tailspin as they try to adjust to change emotionally and physically, but those who have maintained their self-image along the way will always bounce back faster. It's the difference between looking in the mirror and thinking, "I'm a strong, confident woman and I can do this" or looking in the same mirror thinking, "look at me, I'm a mess!" When external issues threaten your sanity, the latter will always push you over the edge.

Just when you think you are getting your act together life will throw you a curveball, every time!

There are a few things that we hear repeatedly that our customers struggle with along life's journey.

Not knowing what to wear

If you do not have clarity on your own style and what suits you, you can find yourself following trends. It is easy to let somebody else make the decisions, but in doing so, you are giving your power to somebody else. You deny yourself the confidence boost that comes with showing up on your terms.

When you are stuck in a rut, it affects everything that you do. It's like you hit pause on living your best life. You live life on default, going from one day to the next, going through the motions. Your inner sparkle is turned down or even worse, goes AWOL and you don't feel confident or inspired. You often feel depressed and the smallest of things has the power to frustrate and irritate you.

Pressure from family to look a certain way

Whether it is sisters, mothers, husbands or daughters, well-intending family members too often tell a woman how to dress, especially if she hasn't made it clear that she has

Just when you think you are getting your act together life will throw you a curveball, every time!

her own preferences. We see it all the time when a woman is shopping for an occasion. She hasn't taken the time to decide what she really likes herself because she is so busy looking after everybody else. Until she takes the time to get a deeper understanding of what she likes herself and gets clarity on how she wants to show up, she will be at the mercy of everybody else's opinion. This can be very overwhelming and disempowering.

Not feeling comfortable or practical

Not feeling comfortable or practical is a distraction. Who wants to be going about their day constantly fixing their clothes or thinking about how their waistband is feeling a bit too tight after they have had lunch? You shouldn't have to think about these things. When you can forget about what you are wearing, you can fully concentrate on the more important things.

Not feeling relevant

Our lifestyles change constantly as we go through life's different stages and we can gather a lot of stuff along the way. When we hit roadblocks, the stuff we have gathered clutters our lives and our minds. If we don't deal with it along the way and stop to take stock, we can end up feeling outdated and irrelevant very quickly.

Not feeling age-appropriate

We have seen this one a million times. From mid-forties on, this is the one we hear most often: "I don't want to dress like my daughter and I certainly don't want to dress like my mother." At this stage, a woman is stuck in the middle. She doesn't know who is catering for her and she has no idea where to start looking. She doesn't want to be mutton dressed as lamb but she also doesn't want to slide into middle age.

You need to hear this – no matter what age you are, you never have to dress old!

What I did about it

That day I stood in my wardrobe, knowing I was well and truly stuck, I decided that I never wanted to feel that way again. It took me a couple of months to get out of that place in my head and move on.

When I overcame it, I wanted to make sure it never happened to my customers, and if it did, I would have a system in place that would help them to get out of it faster than I did. It also changed my focus on how I design my collections.

I continued to give my customers what they wanted, with my own elements of surprise thrown in to excite them, but this new awareness meant my designing became laser-focused on making people feel not only relevant, but

You need to hear this – no matter what age you are, you never have to dress old!

also fabulous, whether they were 30 or 90. As well as designing so that people could forget their flaws and concentrate on their assets, it became my new mission to make sure my customers never got stuck in a rut.

I also developed a simple and clear strategy to evolve constantly over time, inching forward regularly, rather than changing drastically at any one time. It is something that I practice religiously. When I started to share it with other people, it was so simple and I had become so used to doing it, I was surprised to see the intrigue in their faces.

In the coming chapters, I will share with you all of the things I have learned from quietly observing my loyal customers for over 25 years, breaking through my own roadblocks and helping our customers over theirs along the way. I will teach you how to constantly evolve your style so that you always feel confident and relevant, so that when you show up, the sparkle in your eyes is the first thing that people notice.

When you strategically plan your personal style and make a habit of being your most fabulous self every day, you will effortlessly look good and feel great. When you step out of the door every morning as the best version of yourself, that's when the magic in your life happens.

CHAPTER 4

Constantly Evolving is Your Superpower

Why it's important to evolve

Constantly evolving is the key to staying relevant in a fast-paced and changing world. It requires constant reassessing as you go through life. When you invest time in your inner world and know who you are and what you stand for, this is reflected in your outer world. Dressing as an individual is a very way powerful to show up. By the time you walk out of your bedroom in the morning, you've already set yourself up for a great day.

When you dress as an individual, you'll be recognised as being a player rather than an observer, whatever role you may occupy in society.

You'll also be instantly recognisable. People will be able to pick you out in a crowd. They will get to know you for your style and recognise your profile. The people around you will feel secure when you are around. They feel safe when somebody is in control. Even if you are not in a leadership role, sometimes people want to lead, sometimes they want to follow, so you are sending out a signal that you are ready to step up and take on a challenge.

Other people are assured by this, they're inspired by it, they feel confident in you.

However, many women are so busy dealing with busy lives that they don't take the personal time for that inner evolution. In this chapter, I'll run through some of the most common scenarios.

You get stuck when you don't evolve

There are predictable and unpredictable times in every woman's life that will cause emotional and physical distress. These are situations that I have observed happening to my customers over the past 25 years. I have also experienced some of them myself.

You won't experience all of these, but information is power and knowing where these predictable roadblocks may occur will empower you to get through them faster. The inner mastery that comes with the habit of assessing and evolving twice a year, which I am going to walk you through in the following sections, gives you a feeling of control that helps you to get through these tough times. It sounds like a big promise, but when you develop a focused mind, it helps you to think more clearly and calmly in stressful times.

Before we get stuck into the fun stuff, I just wanted to give you a little rundown on the life events that typically catch people out and mess up their heads and their self-confidence and give you a few pointers to successfully evolve through them.

Babies

Evolving through pregnancy

Apart from the normal fluctuations in weight that we all experience right through life, pregnancy is the first time since puberty that you will have to deal with your body drastically changing. Some people love it, but most people really struggle with it.

A mistake that people make is buying maternity clothes that are nothing like the clothes they would normally wear, and as a result, they don't really feel like themselves in them. A pregnancy wardrobe should consist of key pieces that will expand with your bump. This is a time when we get to meet some of our customers for the first time. They don't want to buy maternity clothes but from our jersey collection, they can build a little capsule of pieces that mix and match together to see them through their pregnancy.

I cannot vouch for jersey fabrics across all brands, as a lot of them will not hold their shape as well as ours, but the best jerseys have a really good return, which means that they stretch and stretch but return to their original shape and fit. This means that when your baby bump is gone, you will have pieces that already work in your wardrobe post-baby. During the pregnancy, they can also be layered up with lighter voile pieces and shirt dresses for interest and to create outfits for special occasions.

Evolving post-baby

If you are very lucky, your body will return to close enough its pre-pregnancy shape. However, unfortunately, a lot of people will notice that their hips and boobs have changed forever.

This can be quite stressful and is something that a lot of people struggle with. They may refuse to accept their new body shape and therefore not dress for it, instead they are dressing for the body they had pre-pregnancy. This will not work.

Let it go. Move on with everything that is wonderful about this new stage in your life. It will be different, but in a good way. If there is anything in your wardrobe that doesn't work for you post-baby, put it away somewhere that you don't have to see it. These things may work for you in the future, so hang on to them for now, you can always find new homes for them later. Every woman I have ever met has promised herself that her life will not change when she has kids. The reality is that it does and the quicker you can accept it, the happier you will be.

Your priorities will change as your world starts to revolve around this new little person in your life. You won't have as much time as you had previously, and it is a good idea to have a base wardrobe of pieces that you can wear every day that are easy-care, comfortable and allow you ease of movement.

Choosing pieces for your wardrobe that are comfortable, but still allow you to feel stylish and ready to step out into the world with the least amount of effort as possible will really help you to enjoy this time more.

It is quite easy during the overwhelm of having a new baby to ignore your needs, which does little for your self-esteem. It is a mistake to stay in comfortable loungewear for too long. Some women do this and then don't know where to start when it comes to going back to work or dressing properly.

It's also naive to think you'll have the same amount of time to get ready for work as you did before you had a baby. As you get used to the challenges, stick to easy-care items, so they can be popped into a short wash, hung to dry and will not require ironing.

Your priorities will change as your world starts to revolve around this new little person in your life. You won't have as much time as you had previously, and it is a good idea to have a base wardrobe of pieces that you can wear every day that are easy-care, comfortable and allow you ease of movement.

Evolving with big birthdays

I have always had a problem with the big milestone birthdays. A lot of people celebrate them, I never do. Coming up to them, I always find myself reflecting on what I have done with my life and wondering why I haven't done more! Reaching big birthdays can make us realise that what we wear or what we do isn't working for us. This is because we haven't evolved, we are dressing, acting or thinking like a younger version of ourselves, and somehow haven't caught up. This is especially true if you have a family and have been putting everyone else's needs first, potentially for quite a few years.

I mentioned earlier how I first got stuck in a rut when I hit 40. I hadn't been paying enough attention to myself, I was throwing myself into my family and my work and not really thinking about who I was as a person. I noticed that I didn't really feel passionate about my own sense of style either. I had been coasting for a while, and not evolving my own wardrobe. I was busy doing it for everybody else and I had been neglected. Around the same time as my "wardrobe meltdown", I was at the fabric show in Paris. My heart wasn't in it as I dragged myself around the vast halls of fabrics and trims, which I normally loved. Then, while passing the entrance to one of the stands, I glanced in. Sitting at the bar with a glass of bubbly in her hand, browsing through the collection, was one of the most glamorous

Italian women I have ever seen. She must have been 80. I will never forget that moment, and just like that, I got over being 40. If this woman was still living her dream life at 80, then I still had lots to offer.

When you are constantly evolving your style you always feel relevant, you don't suddenly overnight feel out of date. The other big advantage of evolving your wardrobe over time is that you never have to worry about being age-appropriate.

When you don't evolve regularly, you stick with the same style right through your 30s and into your 40s. Suddenly, you will notice there are a lot of things in your wardrobe that you feel like you cannot wear any more, a top you had in your 20s, a mini skirt that you wouldn't dream of wearing any more. This can happen overnight.

When you evolve your style, season by season, you will always remain relevant. When you get stuck in a style rut, it affects how you see yourself and your self-esteem suffers. This can affect your whole life, including relationships and work. Do not allow yourself to get stuck in a rut!

Evolving through unexpected curveballs

The big birthdays we can prepare for because we can see them coming. It's the unexpected curveballs that sideswipe us when we are not looking that can really take us out of the game for extended stretches of time. When we get a chance to catch our breath, we often realise we are not the same person as we were before.

All of those dramas and unexpected events, from breakups to new relationships, children to health problems, career changes, pivots in life or the loss of a loved one, can leave you feeling wiped and unsure of yourself.

This can have a huge impact on your confidence. We have held the hands of many of our customers through all of these events. The ones who got back on their feet quicker were the ones who invested in their confidence. If they hadn't been doing it already, we got them started, over a cup of coffee, on assessing what worked for them and then developing their wardrobe building habits, which lifted their confidence levels in front of our eyes. So, this stuff does work.

"*I was busy with my clients all year, getting ready for their assessments. Once all the prep-work was finished, I stopped and realised that I felt really stuck. I had not been paying much attention to myself, or making time for me, and it really started to mess with my head. I popped in to have a chat with my favourite stylist, who has become a friend over the years and she really helped me take a step back and assess what I was doing wrong, getting me back on track. I've learned the importance of putting myself first. I can't help others if I don't stay true to myself. You can't pour from an empty cup.*"

-ANONYMOUS-

Keep evolving

The ability to change is what keeps us relevant. The world is changing fast and if we are not on board with embracing change, we can be left behind very quickly.

Change is exciting.

Change is good.

Change allows you to stay passionate... right to the very end.

Section 1 Summary

If you are like me and have got stuck a few times, you will know how it can mess with your head. If you haven't experienced that yet, great; hopefully, this book can prevent it before it happens. Maybe we cannot prevent it every time, but even on those occasions where we find ourselves stuck, we can become more resilient so that we can get unstuck faster. You know now why it is so important to keep moving. Like everything in life, when you don't keep moving you get left behind. Let's not allow that to happen.

Let's move on to the next section where we will discover some of the mistakes that can hold us back and how each step that we take forward will take us closer to eliminating them and becoming more empowered.

SECTION 2

Skip Out the Door Every Morning

"Show up every day like you already have the results, and the universe will deliver"

-MARY GRANT-

Introduction to Section 2

In this section, you will discover the mistakes that we all unconsciously make that result in us spending our money on things that are not right for us. These are the reasons we end up with wardrobes full of things that we don't wear that only serve to clutter our lives and our heads.

I am going to explain why what you wear matters and how it can impact both your physical and mental wellbeing. When you are aware of this, you will already start to make better choices. This will result in you having more energy left at the end of the day and a clearer head for all the more important things like your family, friends and the bigger vision for your life.

You will discover why you should put thought and effort into what you wear every day so that you approach the day inspired. This prepares you to take on the world and achieve everything you want to achieve.

Finally, in this section, we will touch on a subject which is a very big problem in the world, sustainability. I'm not going to go into it in-depth as that is a whole other book. However, it is a topic that concerns everybody and there are simple shifts in our buying habits that we can all make, which require little thought yet can collectively have a huge impact.

CHAPTER 5

7 Mistakes That Cripple Your Style

Why we need to call out these mistakes

I know, I know, nobody likes to hear about the mistakes they make, but it's important that you start to notice mistakes that may be holding you back so we can break the cycle and prevent you from getting stuck in a rut. So, let's just fly through them really quickly. You may recognise some or all of them. Any combination of them can result in a bulging wardrobe of clothes that do not serve you well. These bad habits are the quick fixes that make you buy things that scratch an itch for 5 minutes, but do nothing to make you feel joyful or inspired in the long-term. Understand them and you will be one step closer to building a wardrobe that works for you long-term and, as a result, will only spend your money on things that you get a lot of value out of.

Mistake #1: Following trends

Trends are not gospel. They are merely a reflection of what is happening in the world at that moment. Don't allow them to dictate what you buy. It's a great idea to know what is on-trend, as you can use this information to make sure you are relevant. However, you should curate those trends so that they suit your lifestyle, personality and body shape. If you do the work, your confidence in choosing the pieces that are right for you will already have grown by the time you get to the end of this book, and you will continue to grow as you practise what you learn in the coming chapters. Although you will still value the input of experts who can suggest things that might work for you, you won't need anybody else to tell you what to wear.

Mistake #2: Buying clothes that don't work with what you already have

It's a magpie moment. You spot that bright new shiny thing. You feel an emotional attraction to it, but once you get it home, you wonder what on earth you were thinking. It doesn't work with anything you have already and it just sits there in your wardrobe, like a Billy-no-mates. You keep promising yourself that you will wear it, but it either never happens or you only wear it very rarely because you don't have a variety of ways to wear it.

Mistake #3: Not buying the things you love

Getting over this is one of the best-kept secrets. You cannot truly appreciate it until you break out and do it once. Only then will you see what I mean. How many times have you lusted after a piece that was just 'so you' but didn't buy it, either because you thought it was too expensive or you thought about it so much that you talked yourself out of it? You know, that one piece you still thought about days later? It was a timeless piece you would wear time and time again over its lifetime, but what did you do instead? You opted for a few cheaper, average alternatives and the money was spent anyway. As a result, you either did not wear them or ended up giving them away a few months later.

The next time you find something that you love, think about all the times you will wear it and what the cost per wear will be.

Mistake #4: Waiting for the sales

There are a few problems with this, and they will all leave you feeling disappointed and unfulfilled. We all love to bag a bargain, but it has to be the right bargain and if you only shop in this way, your conscious mind is telling your subconscious that you only deserve the cheap stuff. And, here's the thing, your conscious mind is in charge and your subconscious mind cannot make any decisions to the contrary! Ouch!

Also, when you wait for the sales, you will probably miss out the one piece you really want or your size has been nabbed by the person who walked in the door just before you. We see this all the time in our stores. The other problem with this approach is that you acquire pieces at the end of a season and have little opportunity to wear them until the following year. You would do better to buy your pieces at the start of the season so you can enjoy wearing them, feeling both fabulous and empowered by them all season long. You will reap the rewards many times over.

Mistake #5: Last-minute shopping

This is when a lot of mistakes are made. A last-minute invite or an event has snuck up on you. Suddenly, you are under pressure to get something to wear. This is never a good shopping experience. You will feel the stress of the deadline and rarely enjoy it. You will often end up buying things that you are not in love with.

You will never find things you love when you are shopping under pressure. You will find things that you love when you are relaxed and not looking for anything in particular.

You will usually find more things that you love when you are already feeling inspired and empowered. The right mindset makes all the difference, and as with so many things, like attracts like. When you love what you are wearing, you will always find something else that you love.

Mistake #6: Buying clothes that do not suit your body shape

I've worked with models for 25 years, and I can tell you that every single woman I have ever met (including the models!) has some body issue, something that she doesn't like. We get way too hung up on these things. Too often people shop for the shape and size that they think they will be in 6 months. This is never a good idea. You will only be empowered today by dealing with what you have today. Just get clear on your shape and play down the bits that you do not want to draw attention to.

Mistake #7: Spending too much on outfits for occasions

If there is one thing I could change as a designer who wants to see women being the most confident versions of themselves every day, it is this. Special occasions prompt shopping trips and people end up spending a fortune on things that they only wear once or twice. The rest of the time, they look in their wardrobes and think, "I have nothing

You will never find things you love when you are shopping under pressure. You will find things that you love when you are relaxed and not looking for anything in particular.

to wear." Your clothing budget should be spent according to how often you will wear the pieces you buy. Everyday pieces that make you step out of your front door every day, ready to take on the world are worth investing in.

The way forward

When you dump the 7 mistakes, you will:

- Spend less money
- Spend less time shopping
- Spend less time returning/regretting mistake purchases
- Have more time for more important things
- Have space to breathe in your closet. (Clear your physical space and you'll clear your headspace!)

You will be able to invest more in the things that you really love.

Don't let the mistakes of the past invade your headspace. Too often, we beat ourselves up or waste time justifying things that haven't served us well. Nobody cares, nobody will give it a second thought, only you. So, don't look back, we are not going that way. Forget the mistakes, hold on to the lessons.

CHAPTER 6

Dress to Boost Your Wellbeing

It all starts within

Creating your own individual style is a form of self-mastery. You cannot achieve it without having first assessed who you are, what you like and how you want to show up in the world. Obviously, the sky will not fall down if you do not do this, and only a small percentage of people will. This is good to know, especially if you have a bigger vision as it puts you in the top 5% of people who will show up for what they want. When you know who you are deep down and build out from that place, the world will see and react to you differently. You will show up as somebody who knows where they are going and the universe will deliver!

It is never too early or too late to develop your own style. Whenever you do, you will be free of trends forever. You will be clearer about who you are, what you stand for and you will be more confident in your inner world, which is reflected in your outer world. What you wear every day can influence every aspect of your life. After all, this is the first thing that people see when they meet you and while we shouldn't judge a book by the cover, the reality is that we do. Even if you are not meeting people, you judge yourself when you look in the mirror. Am I right? Put the thought and preparation into what you want your appearance to say and watch how you can make things happen.

This process involves not just putting the work in now, but continually assessing yourself as you go through life, something this book will show you how to do in great detail in the coming chapters.

You don't have to have a lot of clothes to have style, you can have a very distinctive style with surprisingly few pieces. Style is more about attitude than affluence.

When you develop your style, and you tell the world who you are, people will sit up and take notice. They will hear what you have to say. Whatever path you choose in life, this is very desirable. Whether dealing with a partner, children, work colleagues, friends or acquaintances, we all want to be heard and respected.

Don't be invisible and hide behind what other people tell you to wear. Don't be a slave to fashion either, which is a reflection of what is happening at that moment. Be your own person. Develop your own style. Live life on your own terms.

The benefits of developing your style

Here are a few ways that developing your style can have a positive impact on your life.

Invest in your self

Taking the time to develop your personal style gives you a feeling of self-worth, which can spread to other areas as you become more curious about how else you can invest in yourself. It's like an energy that breeds more energy, taking you to other places of personal growth that you never imagined. When I started to become more strategic in what I wore, it gave me so much clarity and headspace I started actively seeking other things that I could use to build on this. It opens your mind to all kinds of other opportunities.

Feel more confident

Being conscious of the clothes that suit you and being able to reassess and quickly adapt as your body changes

Don't be invisible and hide behind what other people tell you to wear. Don't be a slave to fashion either, which is a reflection of what is happening at that moment. Be your own person. Develop your own style.

throughout life gives you a huge confidence boost, and will stop you getting stuck in a negative headspace. It will also prevent you from buying things that do not work for you. You won't buy clothes for the person that you once were or the person that you hope to be in 6 months' time. You will dress for who you are today, making the best of your assets, which you will feel more confident to highlight. Any changes that you might intentionally make are a bonus down the road, but you can still sparkle while you are executing those plans.

We will go into a lot more detail about this in the coming chapters.

Have more time

When you develop your own personal style, you will be more decisive when shopping. You will know what works and what doesn't. There will be less going back and forth making exchanges and you will go on less shopping trips. When this happens, you will suddenly find that you have more time for all the other fun things in life! You will also spend less time thinking about what to wear and less time getting dressed! That's a whole lot of extra time for all the fun stuff!

Improve your mood

We all have days when we wake up and are in a bad mood. These are the days that we need to make the most effort.

Taking a little extra time to do things which will boost your self-esteem, self-worth and confidence, like applying body lotion after your shower or paying a bit more attention to your hair and makeup will make you feel a whole lot better. Even if you only have time for a bit of mascara and lip-gloss, this extra bit of effort will mean you reap the rewards all day.

Be more comfortable

The thinking involved in developing your own style will ensure that you have a wardrobe full of comfortable things. You will eliminate mistakes that end up sitting on the rail. We don't naturally gravitate towards the uncomfortable pieces. We always push them aside in the search for a different option. When you are constantly assessing and evolving, these items will never make it as far as your wardrobe. When you don't have to think about your clothes you will just put them on and forget that they are there, leaving your mind free to think about everything else. This especially applies to footwear.

Nothing will drain your energy as quickly as shoes that leave you crippled by the end of the day. That is a whole lot of lost opportunity right there!

Nothing will drain your energy as quickly as shoes that leave you crippled by the end of the day. That is a whole lot of lost opportunity right there!

Spend more wisely

When you know exactly what works for you and why, you will buy less, which allows you to buy better. Then those investment pieces that you previously only lusted after can be justified. When you buy one quality item that you absolutely love instead of lots of cheaper items, you will keep it for years and get loads of wear out of it, so the cost per wear comes right down. Think how you will feel wearing that one piece that you really wanted that you left behind and then think about all those cheaper less memorable pieces that were purely functional and did nothing for you emotionally when you put them on.

Be in Control

Having your own individual style will give you a feeling of being in control because when you start the day being intentional it becomes harder to shake this, no matter what happens during the day. Having your outfit planned the night before will leave you ready to hit the ground running every morning. Planning your week's outfits in advance is even better. Doing this on a Sunday evening is even more beneficial as it helps you to feel ready to face the week ahead when you wake on Monday mornings.

Being your most confident self allows you to become non-reactive to situations, which instils confidence in the people around you. They know they can rely on you in a crisis. This is invaluable in all situations. You will also feel more in control of your destiny and people will think twice about crossing you!

Reap the rewards

As with everything, you reap what you sow. When you put the work in, you will be effortlessly fabulous. You will enjoy getting dressed because you know that no matter what you put your hand on in your wardrobe, it will just work for you and you will have several options for how you wear it. You will start the day comfortable and inspired. You will have a more positive body image because you know you have put in the work, choosing pieces because they work for you for your own personal reasons. All of this for a little bit of strategic work done twice a year.

You will be your most authentic self.

When those around you know that you have a distinct style that is yours, they are less inclined to tell you what you should wear. Nobody should be allowed to dictate to you how to dress, not even on special occasions. You will remain true to yourself and other people will realise that this is non-negotiable.

CHAPTER 7

Dressing for Success in Everyday Life

"Dress for the result you want to achieve."

-MARY GRANT-

Dressing for success is a phrase that you will most often hear in relation to the corporate world. However, in this chapter, I'm going to show you that dressing for success really applies to all lifestyles. It is about getting into a specific mindset which will result in a successful day, whatever that means on any given day in your life.

Think of how an athlete dresses for peak performance. Imagine if a sprinter tried to run an Olympic race in a suit.

I don't imagine he would pick up any medals because firstly, his mindset would be all wrong and secondly, he wouldn't run as well as he could in his running gear. When you are appropriately dressed, you will always be more aligned for the outcome that you want.

Dressing for success every day is taking this thinking and applying it to everyday situations. There are some basic principles which I will outline below to get you started.

Dressing for success at work

The rules of workwear have changed over the years. In times gone by, people had jobs for life and each job had a uniform. Today that has all changed. Now it is very rare to have a job for life and people are constantly on the move, not just changing the company they work for, but often switching industries. This requires a completely different mindset and people must become much more self-motivated. You need to dress for the outcome that you want to achieve. What you wear affects not just your mindset but how you are perceived, so you really cannot afford to leave it to chance.

Corporate

If this is your work lifestyle, you are most likely well covered for work. There is a very clear and simple dress code for success. If you want to stand out from the crowd, it is tailored, sharp and immaculate. If you want to be at the top, start dressing as if you are already there. People will know that you mean business. When you know where you are going and already act like you are there, you will achieve your goals because you will identify and take the necessary steps, even if you don't know what all those steps are initially. Dressing like you are successful is the first step, which allows you to live that life from the moment you step outside your door.

Business owners/entrepreneurs

The wardrobe of the entrepreneur/business owner is less obvious. It will be dictated by the sector that you are in, but there is great opportunity for you to be individual and stand out from the crowd. It takes a lot of guts to start a business, as you take all the risks and are often the last to reap the rewards. You can have a wardrobe that is a mixture of corporate for important meetings and smart casual or creative for every day because the rules are relaxed. In fact, you write the rules in your world. People will look to you for answers, and you have to be inspired and confident at all times.

Freelancers

About 60% of children in school today will work in jobs that don't exist yet. A portfolio of skills is already replacing the full-time job as we know it today. People are on the move, looking for new challenges and there are great opportunities for people to develop skills that allow them to work remotely. Often freelancers work from home or desk-share part of the time. So, a casual wardrobe is going to hold lots of appeal to this group. However, it is still a good idea to have elements of your wardrobe that you wear on the days when you need to "up your game" or meet clients. It is never a good idea to slip into the habit of not getting dressed and just starting work in your pyjamas. This is detrimental to your self-esteem in the long run.

Creative roles

Very often, working life as a creative is not public-facing so you can get away with wearing anything. However, just because you can does not mean that you should. It is fine to wear whatever it takes to get things done, but special care needs to be taken when you need to be inspired. Whether your role is that of an artist, designer, copywriter, author, musician or any other creative role you can think of, nothing will inspire you quite like wearing your favourite outfits and putting in a little bit of extra effort with your hair and makeup. I often find myself behind the scenes designing the collection and the inspiration just isn't coming. On those occasions, I will always stop and put in a bit of extra effort into my outfit to inspire myself. It gets The Creative juices flowing every time.

Company uniforms

The heroes in the workforce are the teams. Maybe your job requires you to dress in a specific way, either with a dress code or a team uniform which belongs to the company you work for. Don't just throw it on, wear it with pride. This is what you wear for a good chunk of your life and how you wear it affects how you feel about yourself. Wearing it with pride and always having it in immaculate condition not only ensures your most confident self, but also tells people that you care and are committed to your job, which brings all kinds of opportunities.

Dressing for success at home

A strategically planned wardrobe will make sure that you have options that cover both your work life and your time off without having two separate wardrobes. It will also ensure that you don't spend all your money on one at the expense of the other. It is becoming more acceptable these days for work and leisure wardrobes to be the same. You can take the same pieces and combine them in different ways for different emphasis. Sportswear has had a big influence on people's wardrobes, with the growing trend for emphasis being put on being healthier and more active.

It is very important for women raising families to allocate time for themselves so that they keep their own identity.

Sportswear inspired pieces can be very successfully combined with other pieces for smart-casual everyday wardrobes. For example, leggings, trainers and a close-fitting vest can be worn under a shirt dress for a look that will inspire you all day long while allowing you to get things done.

Desk days

We all have them and we very often avoid them like the plague. Desk days are those days when you need to tie yourself to the desk to deal with life administration, reading, writing, creating, or whatever being stuck at a desk means to you. We are inclined to procrastinate a little on those days.

A formula that works for just getting stuck into these activities for me is clear your desk, get a candle, put your favourite music on. Don't wear your lounge clothes, as they will make you want to lounge. Instead, wear something smart but comfy and get your cashmere out or another soft cosy wrap. Even if it is just on the back of your chair, it will set the mood that will make you want to sit at the desk and on cold days, you can throw it around your shoulders and you will feel great. If anything it will make you want to stay at your desk!

Planning days

We all know the key to success and achieving goals is planning. How you dress for your planning days is very important. It doesn't matter whether you are planning for work, life or play, you don't want it to fill up the space you have, you want to just get it done and move on to something more interesting. So, don't hang around in your PJ's lounging on the couch. You need to get in the right frame of mind when smart thinking is required. Wear your most inspiring pieces. Rather than sitting at the kitchen table, use it as an opportunity to go to a coffee shop and be inspired by the world around you. Get out of your comfort zone, whatever it means to you and your individual style, dress to be a badass.

Getting stuff done days

You cannot beat jersey for those 'getting stuff done' days. It is comfortable and you can move in it. We are not suggesting your gym gear here, as that should be reserved for those activities. Think more of mix and match pieces that allow you to move, but also mean you are ready to bump into your worst enemy! You want to look good, but you still want to be able to get stuck in and just get through that to-do list.

These are the days where you don't want to be putting a lot of thought into what you're going to put on when you're getting dressed, so it's good to have a few go-to mix and match outfits. These will allow you to focus on what you have to do, but also leave you ready for unexpected events during the day that call on you to be well put together. Planning these outfits in advance will leave you ready to hit the ground running on these days. To finish off these outfits, I always recommend that you have footwear that allows you to move fast because that in itself is just going to power you through volumes of tasks in a day and leave you with energy leftover instead of feeling worn out.

Family days

When it comes to family life, raising young children and everything that entails, it is very easy to just climb into the nearest thing to hand.

It is very important for women raising families to allocate time for themselves so that they keep their own identity.

When you keep your identity and prioritise time for you, the people around you appreciate you even more and respect that you are a person in your own right. Dressing strategically in easy-care clothes that mix and match will mean that even on your craziest days running after kids or days when the wash basket is overflowing, you will start the day feeling like you are in control of it, rather than it being in control of you.

> "*I'm a teacher. I have a wardrobe of mix and match jersey pieces to which I add a few pieces each season. They work really well for me because I spend most of my day climbing over school bags, but I also have to be ready to meet unexpected visitors to the school.*"
>
> -ORLA REID-
> School Teacher

Dress for the day ysou expect but always be ready for the unexpected.

CHAPTER 8

Sustainability

"The average consumer buys 60% more clothing than 20 years ago. Each garment is kept half as long and about 40% of it is never worn at all."

-UN ECONOMIC COMMISSION FOR EUROPE-

While this is not a book on sustainability, it is such an important subject across every aspect of life that I have to address it. From speaking to people in general, I know that everybody is becoming more and more aware of the importance of making better choices for the good of the planet and the future of our children. Trying to embrace more sustainable practices can be overwhelming all in one go, so the good news is that there are several ways that you can effortlessly step into mindful and sustainable wardrobe buying habits, without having to let it consume you. It's really about making better choices.

Why buy ethically?

The fashion industry is the third most wasteful industry in the world and places a huge demand on raw materials. We need to slow things down and be mindful of what we are buying, how it was produced, how long we will keep it and how we will dispose of it.

Most fashion brands are making changes in how they operate, introducing sustainable lines and improving their practices. I would, however, encourage you to ask questions to make sure that they know you are paying attention. When you know a brand is doing a good job, tell them, spread the word, it will encourage more of the same. Even if you make a small shift in how you shop, it will make a big difference collectively. If you love a brand, but don't love something they have done, stick with them, but give them your feedback. People are inherently good, but we all make bad choices from time to time and we all overlook things that are important when we have a lot to think about.

How to make better buying decisions

If you do not want to go all-in eco, there are various forms of mindful fashion that you can dip into. Remember, all small changes and every contribution makes a difference. Whatever forms of mindful fashion you tap into, you are helping to drive change for good, even if it is only to start with a small percentage of what you buy overall.

Buy from limited production brands

These brands have a policy to never overproduce. Factories have minimum orders and there are hefty surcharges for brands who do not meet them. So the production options are both more limited and more costly for these brands. Support them when you find them. Do not ask them to reduce their price, they will typically only go into sale at the end of a season. They need to make their margins to run their business. If you want to see them around in 3-5 years' time, you must support them today. These are typically the lesser-known brands that you will find in independent boutiques, rather than high street stores which deal in mass production. When you find them, get to know them. They are usually open to feedback, which means that you can have a lot of influence on how they develop and serve you. As a guide, generally brands that produce in Europe do smaller quantities with higher production costs.

They are also well-governed by employment law, so you know everybody in the supply chain has been properly paid for their input. By law, brands must say where the garment was manufactured on the care label, so it's easy for you to check this out.

Invest in high-quality timeless design

There are brands who do not follow trends. They design only pieces that will stand the test of time. They evolve their collections so that you can mix and match pieces from different seasons. The fabrics will be chosen for their quality and the construction of the garments is top-end. You will pay more, but when you work out the cost over several years, these pieces are great value and you will always feel good when you are wearing them.

Accept that custom made should be more expensive

Please be aware that if you pay very little for a special piece which is heavily beaded or embroidered, that does not suggest everybody in the production line was paid fairly. If you want to be responsible and fair when buying for occasions, reduce the detail and go for simple clean lines or pay the price for all the details. I'm sorry if that bursts your bubble, but in this case, if it seems too good to be true, then it absolutely is, there is no probably about it.

Do your homework

Do your research before you shop. If you want to be completely fair and ethical, hunt down the brands that are 100% committed. It will reduce your options, but even if you do it on some pieces, it is worthwhile.

"Demand quality not just in the products you buy, but in the life of the person who made them.

ORSOLA DE CASTRO

Co-founder of Fashion Revolution Day

How to get the most out of the clothes you buy

Buying ethically is part of the solution, but it's what you do with the pieces that you invested in that will really make a difference.

Wear it till it falls apart

Is it really bad to admit that my favourite cashmere wrap has a big hole in it? You would think that I would know somebody who would repair that for me! Worn and loved can be better than brand new. Obviously, this works better with some items than others. Look at the trend for aged and ripped jeans. It has been around for years and it's not going anywhere. Leather jackets are always at their best when they are battered and broken in. To avoid just looking shabby, mix them in with immaculate items for a put-together look with attitude.

Repair, redesign, upcycle

If you are any way handy, this might appeal to you. Psychologically you won't feel the same about your favourite pieces when they are tampered with, but it is a great way to inject a bit of newness or fun into your wardrobe and get the maximum life and value out of pieces that are close to their end of life.

Second hand & vintage

High-quality items have a second-hand value, and you can be very lucky and find pre-loved timeless pieces in vintage and second-hand shops. This may be of particular interest to those who are starting on their fashion journey who have developed an appreciation for quality, but who might not yet have the disposable income to support their taste.

Section 2 Summary

Now you have an awareness of the waste created by mistakes and how they can create clutter in your life. You also understand how what you wear can affect how you feel, both physically and mentally. You know that by showing up for success, you can influence how your day is going to play out. You know how you can be effortlessly sustainable when you make a few small changes.

Knowledge is power. Even if you did not go any further, you are already on the way to making better decisions.

It's about to get interesting now as we start to learn about you in the next section.

SECTION 3

Getting to Know You

"Be yourself, everybody else is taken."

- OSCAR WILDE -

Introduction to Section 3

This is where the fun starts. We are now going to get some clarity around what you like and what suits you.

We will do a fun quiz, which will tell you what your style type is. For this section, I have created style archetypes because sometimes it is easier to see things when we describe somebody other than ourselves. The archetypes are aligned with research I did into different personality types, so as well as helping to identify your style type, I have included lots of information on how you can dip into other style types for different occasions. This means that whatever you are trying to get done in life, your wardrobe has you covered.

You will be able to identify quickly which colour group resonates most with you from the colour vision boards I have created. You will learn about the personalities of the different colours, and how you can use them to influence different situations.

You are also going to find out what body type you are. We know it's a sticking point for everybody as we all have things we don't love about our bodies. However, we are going to learn to accept our good bits and create balance, which makes the most of your assets.

CHAPTER 9

Which Style Archetype Are You?

In this chapter, you are going to work out which one you are.

By merging my observation of the different style types for over 25 years and my research into personality types, I discovered there are 9 style archetypes which sit under three categories.

The categories are:

- **The Thinkers**
- **The Feelers**
- **The Doers**

The Thinkers are:

- *The Trailblazer*
- *The Sophisticate*
- *The Minimalist*

The Feelers are:

- *The Creative*
- *The Bohemian*
- *The Romantic*

The Doers are:

- *The Rock Chick*
- *The Provider*
- *The Athlete*

For the book, I have created a fun quiz which will tell you which one you are. You can check it out here: ***https://marygrant.com/style-archetype-quiz/***

Of course, various archetypes will come out to play on different occasions and while one will be dominant you will notice that there are others you also identify with. It is useful to know what the personality traits and uses of each of the others are so that you can call on them for different situations.

In this chapter, I will tell you about the archetypes and how you can use the various ones to your advantage. Try and visualise the character that I am describing outside of yourself as this makes it much easier to identify which one is most like you.

Each archetype has very strong identifying personality traits. When you know what they are, you will be able to spot the different archetypes, which is also a fun people-watching activity.

You can aspire to any of the archetypes, especially if you want to change any aspect of your life. If you want to cultivate a new archetype, start with a couple of key pieces, pay attention to the people you admire and build your collection over time. Like everything else, being successful at combining different archetypes requires practice. When you want to introduce a new type, practice when nobody is looking. Get into the character around the house so it becomes effortless in public. Don't adopt a different character for a special occasion as you will just end up looking and feeling uncomfortable.

When you understand the personality traits of each of the archetypes, you can dip into them at different times to influence your mindset and inspire yourself.

The Thinkers

The Sophisticate | The Trailblazer | The Minimalist

The Thinkers are very often in leading roles and are known to be more interested in big ideas than mundane and practical activities. They have a clear and identifiable no-nonsense approach to their personal style and often don't understand or get the more touchy-feely archetype styles. They mix well with The Doer archetypes for down-time and need to ensure some of their wardrobe will allow them to switch off.

The Sophisticate

Signature traits

Sharp | Polished | Chic | Traditional | Glamorous

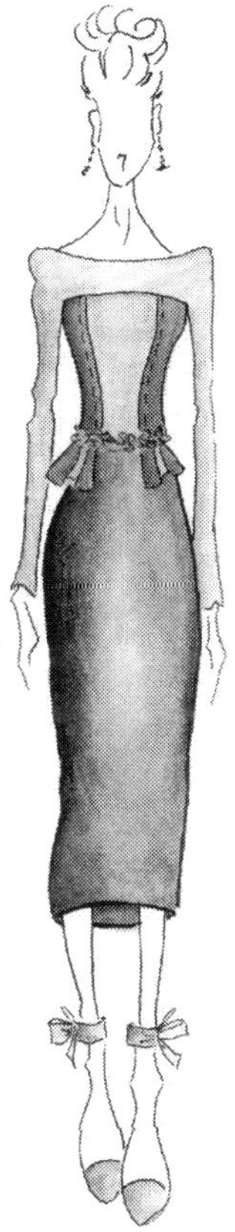

Check out The Sophisticate vision board here:
https://www.pinterest.ie/marygrantdesigner/the-sophisticate/

The Sophisticate exudes power and style. She is comfortable in the role of a leader and people look up to her and admire her from near and far. She is immaculate. Her clothes, hair, makeup and general grooming is effortlessly polished because this is how she shows up every day. She takes her career and future seriously. She is focused on the destination and often knows exactly how she is going to get there.

She is attracted to both classic and modern styles. She appreciates fine tailoring, structure and clean well-cut lines. She may be partial to a bit of embellishment, but it is always understated. You will recognise her for her tailored coats, dresses and minimal classic jewellery. She appreciates no-nonsense clothes that require little thought. She just wants to put them on and go. This archetype does not typically favour either neutrals or colour in her wardrobe. The simplicity for her is in one or two-piece outfits that do not require any thought.

The Sophisticate's wardrobe is perfectly suited to business because it requires little thought from day to day once it has initially been put together. Wardrobe staples do not change from season to season and The Sophisticate chooses quality classic pieces that do not date. When she is not attracted to every bright new shiny thing, she can allocate more of her budget to higher-quality items that will stand the test of time.

As her wardrobe is not typically seasonal, The Sophisticate needs to be mindful of staying current and adjust her styling promptly as the seasons change. She will need to be intentional about bringing out her softer side when it comes to family and romance. This will also help her to unwind and gives her head some much-needed rest.

Some cosy knits and perhaps some cashmere would be great to help her to wind down at the weekends. As The Sophisticate tends to mostly wear heels and frequently carries a bag on her arm, she may suffer from backache at the end of the day and can run out of energy when the other archetypes have energy left over. She should be mindful to swap her heels for flat shoes when she can and keep that handbag light!

If you are this archetype, mix it with:
The Romantic *when you want to bring out your softer side.*
The Provider *when you want to get stuff done.*

The Sophisticate shopping list

- ✓ *Elegant tailored coats and overcoats*
- ✓ *Tailored jackets*
- ✓ *Leather jackets*
- ✓ *Shift dresses*
- ✓ *Little black dresses*
- ✓ *Wrap dresses*
- ✓ *Crew-neck sweaters*
- ✓ *Wrap shirts*
- ✓ *Simple white T-shirts*
- ✓ *Pencil skirts*
- ✓ *Skinny jeans*
- ✓ *Tailored trousers*
- ✓ *Black pumps*
- ✓ *Elegant flats*

- ✓ *Ankle boots*
- ✓ *Classic handbags*
- ✓ *Sunglasses*
- ✓ *Classic watch and jewellery*
- ✓ *Assorted scarves*
- ✓ *Strong colour lipstick*

The Trailblazer

Signature traits

Futuristic | individual | creative | unconventional | considered

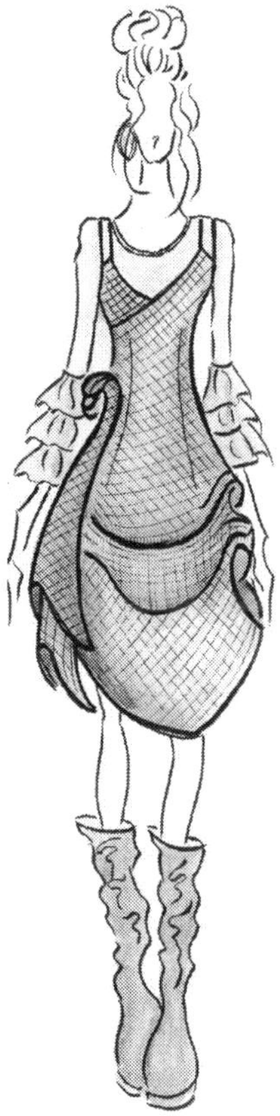

Check out The Trailblazer vision board.

https://www.pinterest.ie/marygrantdesigner/the-trail-blazer/

The Trailblazer is a thought leader. It is not important for her to be thought of in that way, as she will do her own thing no matter who is looking. She is known to be fast-paced and moves on quickly from everything, including the crap that life can throw at her. Her style is eye-catching and much admired by those around her who often look to her for inspiration. She is futuristic and can often be extravagant in her appearance. She likes to push the boundaries of convention in all areas of her life.

She is attracted to shapes that are conceptual, expressive, bold and lend themselves to layering for an original and edgy look. She is not overly concerned with showing off her body in the same way as some of the other archetypes are. Rather, she has a private, personal relationship and connection to her clothes. She is attracted to quality and unusual items and has the most individual of all wardrobes. While she may favour monochrome outfits – there are lots of blacks, whites, greys and metallics to be found in her wardrobe – she may also be partial to occasional bursts of colour.

The Trailblazer wardrobe inspires creative thinking. She has a great eye for individual items that mix and match, so her wardrobe will organically have lots of versatile options. For her, evolving comes naturally.

Her edgy style can be a little bit intimidating for others, especially if they are not so style-conscious. The Trailblazer might want to be mindful of softening her look when she wishes to connect with mere mortals.

The Trailblazer likes to be edgy, but timeless, choosing pieces that are less trend-driven and speak to her personality.

If you are this archetype, mix it with:
The Romantic *when you want to bring out your softer side and* ***The Rock Chick*** *or* ***The Athlete*** *when you want to get stuff done.*

The Trailblazer shopping list

- ✓ *Unusual coats*
- ✓ *Quirky jackets*
- ✓ *Leather jackets*
- ✓ *Unstructured dresses*
- ✓ *Structured dresses*
- ✓ *Layering dresses*
- ✓ *Dramatic, iconic pieces*
- ✓ *Statement accessories*
- ✓ *Interesting textures and shapes*
- ✓ *Tunics*
- ✓ *Layering base layers*
- ✓ *Contrasting cuts*
- ✓ *Modern cuts*
- ✓ *Exaggerated ruffles and frills*
- ✓ *Asymmetrical hemlines*
- ✓ *Anything unusual and versatile*
- ✓ *Metallic and chunky accessories*
- ✓ *Knitwear*
- ✓ *Anything tulle*
- ✓ *Attention to details, zippers, hardware, stitching, etc.*

The Minimalist

Signature traits

Mindful | timeless | simplicity | immaculate | quality

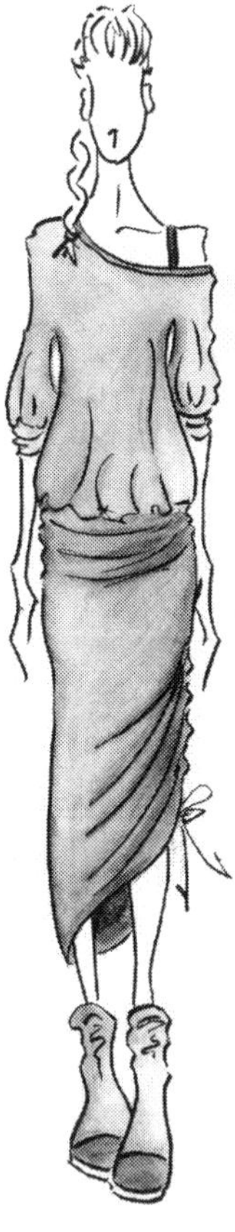

Check out The Minimalist vision board here:
https://www.pinterest.ie/marygrantdesigner/the-minimalist/

The Minimalist knows that a clear space means a clear head. She is a deep and conceptual thinker who often comes up with brilliant ideas. She cannot think straight in the presence of clutter and everything, from her kitchen to her wardrobe will reflect that. As she is more concerned with big futuristic ideas, the simplicity of this archetype allows her to spend less time on the practical and mundane elements of life. She typically shops when she doesn't need to and finds her best pieces when she is browsing.

She has a keen eye for detail and appreciates quality fabrics in mix and match pieces that will give her lots of versatile wardrobe options. She likes clean, unfussy lines and naturally gravitates towards clothes that are multi-functional and timeless. Her look is always pared-back, less is more with The Minimalist. Where others might pile on the accessories, she will typically remove an item before she heads out the door. She favours neutral colours which mix and match effortlessly.

This wardrobe is great for creative thinking. Simplicity creates headspace which is the perfect environment for big ideas to form. While she may have less quantity in her wardrobe than the other archetypes, The Minimalist typically chooses quality pieces that work well together, so always has lots of options. She is very clear and intentional in her choices, so you will rarely find waste or mistakes in her wardrobe.

The Minimalist is very practical and likes to get lots of wear out of her clothes, so she may find the choices in her wardrobe are quite limited when it comes to evenings or special occasions. A good option for her is to make sure that she has a few simple dresses or one colour mix and match separates that can be dressed up with statement jewellery.

The Minimalist needs to intentionally evolve her wardrobe regularly, even if it is just to make small changes, as The Creative mind gets bored if things stay the same for too long. This archetype mixes very well with some tougher elements of The Rock Chick to keep things interesting.

If you are this archetype, mix it with:
The Bohemian *or* ***The Romantic*** *when you want to bring out your softer side and* ***The Athlete*** *when you want to get stuff done.*

The Minimalist shopping list

- ✓ *Neutral colours*
- ✓ *Clean lines*
- ✓ *Quality fabrics*
- ✓ *Natural fabrics*
- ✓ *Unstructured coats*
- ✓ *Unstructured jackets*
- ✓ *Great knits*
- ✓ *Unstructured dresses*
- ✓ *Modern shapes*
- ✓ *Pinafores*
- ✓ *Dungarees*
- ✓ *Layering pieces*
- ✓ *White shirts*
- ✓ *Jersey dresses*
- ✓ *T-shirts*
- ✓ *Skinny tops*

- ✓ *Cropped trousers*
- ✓ *Leggings*
- ✓ *Timeless shoes*
- ✓ *Ankle boots*
- ✓ *Loafers*
- ✓ *Brogues*
- ✓ *White trainers*
- ✓ *Understated bags*
- ✓ *Simple Sunglasses*
- ✓ *Jewellery can be simple or quirky*
- ✓ *Scarves*

The Feelers

The Bohemian | The Creative | The Romantic

These are the intuitive archetypes. They are people people and are warm, considerate and nurturing. They are the givers, carers, musicians, artists and counsellors. The feeler archetypes appreciate comfort and have interesting, soft, often ethereal wardrobes. They might want to dip into The Thinker archetypes when they want to be taken more seriously.

The Bohemian

Signature traits

Vintage | distinctive | colourful | carefree | natural

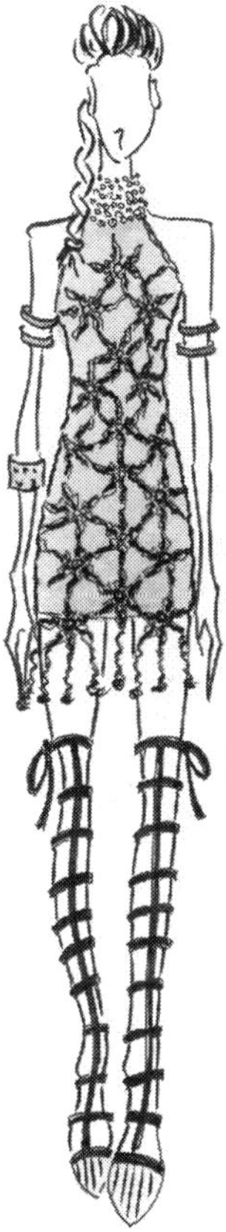

Check out The Bohemian vision board.

https://www.pinterest.ie/marygrantdesigner/the-bohemian/

This is the most carefree of all the archetypes. The Bohemian is a visionary. She is idealistic, ethical and highly principled. She has an artistic and unconventional lifestyle and oozes creativity and imaginative ideas. She dreams of a better world and champions worthy causes. She does not live in the past, but rather prefers to imagine what could happen in the future. Her carefree and easy-going attitude creates a sense of peace and calm, both in herself and the people around her. She is seen as very approachable and people open up to her easily.

The Bohemian has an innate sense of personal style. She effortlessly combines textures and colours. She likes to mix things from different eras and may be a regular visitor to vintage and pre-loved stores, where she finds gems that others might not even look at twice. She effortlessly puts outfits together that would look ridiculous on others, but they just look right on her. She doesn't like clothes that restrict her and likes the freedom of long flowing pieces and loose layers. She loves soft earthy colours which she combines effortlessly into individual and imaginative outfits.

Because vintage and pre-loved often make her heart beat faster, she can get a lot of mileage out of her wardrobe budget. Her look is unique and impossible to copy because she has a knack for finding pieces that are not readily available. Her buying habits effortlessly contribute to sustainability which is very important to her.

This archetype is perfect in creative environments but may find it uncomfortable on occasions when she needs to step into more conventional business-type situations. She can be prepared by having a few classic timeless structured pieces that can be called on when the need arises.

The Rock Chick style mixes really well with this style, toughening it up and giving it lots of attitude.

If you are this archetype, mix it with:
The Trailblazer *when you want to be more serious.*
The Rock Chick *or* ***The Athlete*** *when you want to get stuff done.*

The Bohemian shopping list

- ✓ *All things vintage*
- ✓ *Velvet coats*
- ✓ *Embroidered coats*
- ✓ *Aviator jackets*
- ✓ *Long knitted cardigans*
- ✓ *Waistcoats and vests*
- ✓ *Denim or fur jackets*
- ✓ *Romantic maxi dresses*
- ✓ *Unstructured and oversized tunics, shirts and blouses*
- ✓ *Flowing maxi skirts*
- ✓ *Flared jeans*
- ✓ *Neutral coloured ankle boots*
- ✓ *Tie-dye*
- ✓ *Suede*
- ✓ *Prints*
- ✓ *Crochet*
- ✓ *Lace*
- ✓ *Bandanas*
- ✓ *Gladiator sandals*
- ✓ *Floppy brimmed hats*

- ✓ *Wide-brimmed hats*
- ✓ *Scarves that can double up as headbands*
- ✓ *Also, large printed scarves*
- ✓ *Chunky earth jewellery*
- ✓ *Accessories with fringing*
- ✓ *Fringing*
- ✓ *Aviators sunglasses*
- ✓ *Gladiator sandals*
- ✓ *Cowboy boots*
- ✓ *Belts*
- ✓ *Cross body bags*
- ✓ *Layered jewellery*
- ✓ *Crystals and gemstones*

The Creative

Signature traits

Artistic | fun | inventive | details | colourful

Check out The Creative vision board.
https://www.pinterest.ie/marygrantdesigner/the-creative/

The Creative archetype is fun and adventurous. The world sees her as artistic and unconventional. She is passionate and loves to try new things, inspiring those around her to do the same. She has creative hobbies and likes to wear clothes that express her creative personality. She often likes to make her own clothes and accessories and is interested in all things crafted and handmade. She avoids conventional dressing and likes to create a look that is unique to her.

She likes to experiment and is drawn to new trends, which speak to her love of art and creativity. She likes lots of colour and has lots of variety in her eclectic wardrobe. She likes to champion creative people and incorporates their wares into her unique style.

There is a lot of colour in her wardrobe, which provides an endless supply of daily inspiration. She spreads joy wherever she goes.

As with the other 'feeler' archetypes, The Creative needs to be mindful to include some items in her wardrobe that she can call on for more serious occasions, especially if she is aiming for a promotion or to be taken seriously in a business environment.

If you are this archetype, mix it with:
The Sophisticate *when you want to be more business-like.*
The Provider *when you want to get stuff done.*

The Creative shopping list

- ✓ *Anything patchwork*
- ✓ *Applique*
- ✓ *Lots of colour*
- ✓ *Interesting prints*
- ✓ *Art on clothes*
- ✓ *Colourful coats*
- ✓ *Versatile knitwear*
- ✓ *Oversized dresses*

- ✓ *Layered dresses*
- ✓ *Pinafores*
- ✓ *Dungarees*
- ✓ *Maxi dresses*
- ✓ *Floaty layers*
- ✓ *Kaftans*
- ✓ *Handmade jewellery*
- ✓ *Scarves that can double as headgear*
- ✓ *Art on shoes*
- ✓ *Trainers*
- ✓ *Colourful shoes*
- ✓ *Coloured handbags*
- ✓ *Art on handbags*
- ✓ *Crafted jewellery*
- ✓ *Cross body bags*
- ✓ *Ceramic and gemstone jewellery*
- ✓ *Sunglasses*

The Romantic

Signature traits

Soft | feminine | delicate | adaptable | floaty

Check out The Romantic vision board.

https://www.pinterest.ie/marygrant-designer/the-romantic/

The Romantic archetype is warm and approachable and a real people person. Winter or summer, she prefers soft feminine outfits. She is drawn to ethereal flowing shapes, draped fabrics and soft knits, ruffles and lace. Summer is her time to shine, but she still manages to be soft and feminine even on the darkest winter days, bringing peace and tranquillity to those around her. She is generous and loves nothing more than to give back. She likes harmony and teamwork and brings out the best in others. She is a carer and nurturer and is seen as being easy-going, kind and loving. She can be a bit of a day-dreamer and is very popular among all the other archetypes. Attracting love interests is a breeze for her and she is the archetype that the others should pay attention to when in the same situation!

She loves lace, floating fabrics and soft pastel colours. She often likes to layer chiffons, silks and tactile jerseys will be very attractive to her. Even in a work situation, there is often a bit of lace lurking somewhere in her outfit. When she wants to add a bit of edge to her look, The Rock Chick is a perfect complementary style.

The Romantic has lots of variety in her wardrobe and has plenty of choice for downtime, occasions and social environments.

Because she is drawn to soft dreamy wardrobe pieces, she will need to calculate her needs and be mindful to plan her workwear wardrobe for balance.

If you are this archetype, mix it with:
The Minimalist *or* ***The Sophisticate*** *when you want to be more business-like.* ***The Rock Chick*** *or* ***The Athlete*** *when you want to get stuff done or feel more grounded.*

The Romantic shopping list

- ✓ *Softly tailored coats*
- ✓ *Leather jackets*
- ✓ *Softly tailored jackets*
- ✓ *Cashmere wraps*

- ✓ *Knitwear layered*
- ✓ *Oversized shirt dresses in lightweight fabrics*
- ✓ *Lace dresses*
- ✓ *Layering outfits*
- ✓ *All things velvet from coats to boots*
- ✓ *All white outfits*
- ✓ *Pretty floral prints*
- ✓ *Floaty chiffons and voiles*
- ✓ *Sheer embroideries*
- ✓ *Lace tops*
- ✓ *Unstructured shirts*
- ✓ *Ruffles and flounces*
- ✓ *Pastel colours and prints*
- ✓ *Colourful shoes and sandals*
- ✓ *Faux fur*
- ✓ *Tulle*
- ✓ *Coloured heeled boots*
- ✓ *Nude court shoes*
- ✓ *Anything Velvet*
- ✓ *Pretty jewellery*
- ✓ *Floral accessories*
- ✓ *Pretty hair accessories*

The Doers

The Provider | The Rock Chick | The Athlete

The Doer archetypes are the most practical group. They typically like to dress more casually, and like to get stuck in and get things done. They might like to dip into The Thinker archetype group when they want to inspire themselves and The Feeler group in order to bring out their more feminine side.

The Provider

Signature traits

Comfortable | practical | understated | lifestyle | everyday

Check out The Provider vision board here.

https://www.pinterest.ie/marygrantdesigner/the-provider/

The Provider archetype is the one who likes to get things done. She will be the one who has her sleeves rolled up and is halfway through the task while others are still thinking about it. She is quite happy to work on her own, and can move mountains when she is in her stride. She is the dependable friend in times of need, and will always make time to help other people get their stuff done too. You know how the saying goes, 'when you want something done, ask the busiest person in the room' – that's her. She is brilliant at developing and implementing plans and strategies.

She is not a big fan of fuss or frills. She likes practical clothes that she can wear every day and are easily cared for.

Her wardrobe is full of comfortable mix and match pieces that allow her to hop effortlessly between various activities.

The Provider favours a low-maintenance wardrobe and is a non-fussy shopper who will save her time for other more important things.

The Provider needs to be careful not to slip into the habit of wearing jeans and hoodies all the time as this is the fastest route to becoming invisible.

If you are this archetype, mix it with:
The Sophisticate *when you want to be more business-like.*
The Romantic *when you want to bring out your feminine side.*

The Provider shopping list

- ✓ *Mix and match neutral or soft colours*
- ✓ *Leather jackets*
- ✓ *Aviator jackets*
- ✓ *Blazer jacket*
- ✓ *Denim jacket*
- ✓ *Bomber jackets*
- ✓ *Down jackets and vests*
- ✓ *Easy knitwear*
- ✓ *Hoodies*

- ✓ *Cardigans*
- ✓ *Casual dresses*
- ✓ *Relaxed fit dresses*
- ✓ *Classic shirts and blouses*
- ✓ *Plaid shirts*
- ✓ *White shirts*
- ✓ *Pinafores*
- ✓ *Dungarees*
- ✓ *Jeans*
- ✓ *Leggings*
- ✓ *Softly tailored trousers*
- ✓ *Jersey tops*
- ✓ *T-shirts*
- ✓ *Various skirts from straight to A-line, knee-length to 3/4 length*
- ✓ *Bold accessories*
- ✓ *Vintage store and grandma's attic finds*
- ✓ *White trainers*
- ✓ *Converse*
- ✓ *Ankle boots*
- ✓ *Dr Martens*
- ✓ *Knee-high boots*

- ✓ *Practical holdall bag*
- ✓ *Practical cross body bag*
- ✓ *Hats and caps*
- ✓ *Sunglasses*

The Rock Chick

Signature traits

Attitude | edgy | confident | spirited | tough

Check out The Rock Chick vision board.

https://www.pinterest.ie/marygrantdesigner/the-rock-chick/

The Rock Chick archetype is edgy and full of attitude. She is confident in her own skin and can come across as being a tough nut when the reality is she usually has a soft centre. She is extroverted with strong people skills and a great communicator. She likes to experience new things and happily shares her learning with others. She is friendly, fun and happy to be the centre of attention, while still being sensitive to other people's needs.

She has a laid-back attitude to dressing and favours jeans, leather jackets, biker boots, which she prefers when they are well broken in. The more aged her leather jacket is the more she will love it. She is attracted to hardware trims and often pinches her boyfriend's/husband's knits, jewellery and watches, which fit perfectly into her edgy style. She favours great knits which add a softer dimension to her look.

This is a great lifestyle wardrobe that allows The Rock Chick to get things done without her fading into the background.

When she wants to soften her look, The Rock Chick combines well with the softer elements of The Romantic. Lace elements and softer fabrics will work beautifully with her leather jackets, knitwear, skinny jeans and leggings.

One of the advantages of being The Rock Chick is that you can create your own individual looks by distressing jeans and cutting long dresses up into shorter versions with asymmetrical hems. The more creative and worn the better.

This archetype loves mixing unexpected combinations, like flirty dresses with biker boots and satin dresses with leather jackets, combining different fabric textures from knits to metallics.

If you are this archetype, mix it with:
The Sophisticate *or* ***The Minimalist*** *when you want to be more business-like and* ***The Romantic*** *when you want to bring out your feminine side.*

The Rock Chick shopping list

- ✓ *Overcoat*
- ✓ *Leather jacket*
- ✓ *Denim jacket*
- ✓ *Aviator jacket*
- ✓ *Boyfriend's jumpers*
- ✓ *Chunky knit jumpers*
- ✓ *Chunky knit cardigans*
- ✓ *All things studded*
- ✓ *Faux fur gilets*
- ✓ *Asymmetrical dresses*
- ✓ *Vintage dresses*
- ✓ *Lace overdresses*
- ✓ *Lace skirts*
- ✓ *Black Tulle over pieces*
- ✓ *Black tulle skirt*
- ✓ *Lace trim camis*
- ✓ *White shirts*
- ✓ *White oversized T-shirts*
- ✓ *Concert T-shirts*
- ✓ *Jeans*

- ✓ *Leather skirts*
- ✓ *Wet look leggings*
- ✓ *Skinny jeans*
- ✓ *Stiletto ankle boots*
- ✓ *Studded boots*
- ✓ *Dr Martens*
- ✓ *White trainers*
- ✓ *Converse*
- ✓ *Hats*
- ✓ *Edgy jewellery*
- ✓ *Boyfriend jewellery*
- ✓ *Neckties*
- ✓ *Chokers*
- ✓ *Oversized handbags*
- ✓ *Studded belts*
- ✓ *Rock star sunglasses*

The Athlete

Signature traits

Sporty | modern | understated | relaxed | body conscious

Check out The Athlete vision board.
https://www.pinterest.ie/marygrantdesigner/the-athlete/

This is the most body-conscious archetype. She is always mindful of her health and fitness and is drawn to sporty and sport-inspired clothes. She is full of energy and always on the go. The other archetypes will often find it hard to keep up with her, and she will still be on the go when the rest have collapsed in a heap. She needs social interaction and is a great team player. She likes to make life up as she goes along and believes that action is better than perfection.

The Athlete doesn't like to be pinned down and will always choose comfort over style. She loves stretch in everything and feels restricted in structured and fitted non-stretch clothes.

The ever-increasing trend towards health and wellness means that the athleisure trend that she favours is going nowhere. Also, with a big shift in how people work, with the gig economy and freelancers becoming more popular, this style type has slipped into normal everyday workwear.

The Athlete will always want to spend her money on more sporty clothes, so she needs to be intentional and plan for other demands on her wardrobe. She may well have to be wrestled away from her gym leggings, so switching them up for a less sporty version and layering them up with relaxed pieces from other style types is a great option for a more versatile wardrobe which allows her to be taken seriously. This archetype works particularly well when combined with Rock Chick pieces.

If you are this archetype, mix it with:
The Minimalist *or* ***The Sophisticate*** *when you want to be more business-like.* ***The Romantic*** *when you want to bring out your feminine side.*

The Athlete shopping list

- ✓ *Leather jacket*
- ✓ *Denim jacket*
- ✓ *Rain jacket*
- ✓ *Neoprene jackets*

- ✓ *Oversized hoody*
- ✓ *Fitted hoody*
- ✓ *Oversized knitwear*
- ✓ *Oversized shirt dresses*
- ✓ *Skinny jersey dresses*
- ✓ *Cutout tops*
- ✓ *Soft wrap cardigans*
- ✓ *Soft easy fit dresses for over leggings*
- ✓ *Tracksuit bottoms*
- ✓ *Leggings*
- ✓ *Short skirts for over leggings*
- ✓ *College T-shirts*
- ✓ *Cropped hoodies*
- ✓ *Oversized T-shirts*
- ✓ *Bralets*
- ✓ *Shorts*
- ✓ *High denier tights*
- ✓ *Gym wear leggings and tops*
- ✓ *Gym shoes*
- ✓ *Dance inspired tops*
- ✓ *Walking boots*
- ✓ *Chunky socks*

- ✓ *Dr Martens*
- ✓ *Converse*
- ✓ *Skinny jeans*
- ✓ *Oversize holdall*
- ✓ *Caps*
- ✓ *Chunky scarves*
- ✓ *Sunglasses*

Your unique style

This was one of the most fun chapters to write. Every time I read it I get excited again about the possibilities. Your style archetype is your starting point for building your personal style. The fun really starts when you throw in a little bit of influence from the other archetypes you are attracted to. Remember, there are no rules, only guidelines which you can follow until you become comfortable enough to push your boundaries a little. At no time will I be telling you what to wear. The aim is to empower you to recognise what you are most drawn to and to create your own iconic style by strategically combining the things that you love the most.

If you would like to explore personality types further, I found this is a great place to start.

https://opensource.com/open-organization/16/7/personality-test-for-teams

CHAPTER 10

The Witchcraft of Colour Psychology

The power of colour

We all have favourite colours, even if they do not feature in our wardrobes. Each colour has a character, so knowing what these are and how they can be used in everyday situations is very powerful. Imagine being able to diffuse difficult situations just by wearing a certain colour. When you are finished with this chapter, you might just change how you think about colour. You may even find yourself dabbling in a bit of witchcraft!

It is quite likely that you will favour one particular group of colours in your wardrobe. If you stick to this one group, you will find that your individual garments work better together. This works especially well for building a capsule collection because when you throw in random colours, which do not work with several other pieces in your wardrobe, they will just sit on the rail disrupting your view of your outfit options.

You can always inject a little of a secondary group if you like, but just be mindful when doing so that your wardrobe doesn't end up looking like a car crash.

Which colour type are you?

As with the previous section on knowing your style type, I have created vision boards to help you get clarity on the colour group that you identify most with. Once you know your colour type, you can become much more focused on what you allow into your wardrobe.

1. Neutral colours

Black | white | grey | brown | naturals | metallics

Check out our board here and see if this is the colour group that speaks to you:
https://www.pinterest.ie/marygrantdesigner/the-neutral-colours/

2. *Soft & earthy colours*

Pastels | whites | stones & sands | blue | green | the colours of nature

Check out our board here and see if this is the group that speaks to you:
https://www.pinterest.ie/marygrantdesigner/soft-earthy-colours/

3. *Vibrant colours*

Red | yellow | orange | strong blues, greens, pinks | neons

Check out our board here and see if this is the group that speaks to you:
https://www.pinterest.ie/marygrantdesigner/vibrant-colours/

Specific colours and how to wear them

Black

Sophisticated | serious | intelligent

People who wear black are seen as being serious and diligent. They are also often sensitive and emotional although they can come across as being quite tough and will not always admit it. If you wear black a lot, people will often tell you not to buy more black. We hear it so often when people come into our stores. And what do they end up buying? Yes, more black! It is by far the most popular colour in fashion, sorry guys! Black will always be the new black!

Tips for wearing black

- Wear it when you want to impress!
- Have a little black dress, even if it's the only piece of black in your wardrobe. It will see you dressed for any formal occasion.
- Add pops of colour to soften black and add interest.
- Be aware that as we get older, our complexion changes and all black can look quite harsh, so keep an eye on it and soften it as you get older, especially if you favour dying your hair black.
- Be careful of black if you tend to have dark shadows under your eyes as black close to your face can accentuate them.
- Wear black tourmaline gemstones to keep you grounded and to clear negativity.

White

Meticulous | free | pure

White is the colour of cleanliness, innocence and purity. Wearing it implies that you are an organised and detail-oriented person. Some old rules about wearing white suggest that it can only be worn in the summer. It can be worn all year round, just be selective in the pieces that you wear; for example, a white shirt is always going to work and winter white always looks great, even on the most wintery days.

Tips for wearing white

- Wear it colour blocked with black for dramatic, powerful outfits.
- If you find that it can wash you out, break it up with other colours.
- Wear plain undergarments that match your skin tone, leave the patterns and lace at home.
- Everyone can wear white, you just need to find the right one for your skin tone.
- Apply your perfume before getting dressed and your makeup after getting dressed to avoid staining.
- Wear white selenite gemstones to release stuck energy and achieve balance.

Grey

Balanced | tranquil | dimensional

Grey is one of those neutral colours that, on its own, does not define somebody's personality. However, if you wear a lot of grey, you may fade into the background. It can be seen as the colour of maturity or somebody flying under the radar. It does work well in a wardrobe of neutral colours and blacks. It also looks incredible on people with grey hair, especially when worn with soft pinks and lavenders.

Tips for wearing grey

- Wear it with darker or intense colours.
- Wear it with a pop of colour in your accessories.
- Wear it with soft pinks and neutral peachy colours for a sophisticated look.
- Be careful of wearing pale greys from head to toe, it could end up looking drab.
- Colour block with black for a sophisticated but softer look than head to toe black.
- Wear grey moonstone gemstones to enhance intuition and patience and get in touch with your more feminine side.

Brown

Reliable | peaceful | strength

Brown is the colour of the earth, so people who wear it are seen as being earthy calm and grounded. They are quite conservative and respectful of other people. They seek peace and stability. They are seen by others as being rational and intelligent.

Tips for wearing brown

- Wear it in situations when you want to be seen as being strong, reliable and trustworthy.
- Mix it with colours like orange and yellow for harmony.
- Brown and beige are a natural pairing that never goes out of style.
- Mixed with white, brown is very chic.
- Don't use too much of the same tone, mix it with some black details to spice it up.
- Wear brown tiger's eye gemstones to reduce overwhelm, become unreactive in stressful situations and to stay centred.

Blue

Kind | trustworthy | tranquil

Navy is a great softer alternative to black, especially in the summer. Blue is known to slow down human metabolism and have a calming effect on the psyche. Often if you ask people what their favourite colour is they will say blue. It is the colour of the sky, the colour of the sea, it is everywhere in nature and is associated with peace and tranquillity. It has a peaceful effect on people around you. This is also the reason that a lot of people use it in bedrooms.

Tips for wearing blue

- Navy is a great softer alternative to black, especially in summer.
- Wear for interviews as is says confidence and reliability.
- Wear navy with bright whites for a very sharp and chic look.
- Wear darker shades of blue when you want to have a calming effect.
- Wear navy and pale blues for business to inspire confidence.
- Wear it when you are feeling stressed as it has a calming effect.
- Wear blue larimar gemstones when you want to promote peace, confidence and clear communication.

Green

Caring | pleasant | peaceful

The colour of nature, green is calming and easy on the eye. It can also be seen as the colour of envy and greed, so be careful not to wear too much of it. It is not the colour to wear if you want to set the world on fire, but on the other hand, green is also seen as the colour of luck, so wear it if you are feeling a little bit superstitious. It can also mean you are full of life, healthy and environmentally aware. It is the colour used for a lot of eco-friendly products and is also the colour of healing.

Tips for wearing green

- Don't wear head-to-toe green in a work situation if you are looking for a promotion, you will fade into the background.
- Wear it with florals for a fresh springtime look.
- Added as a pop of colour to black, it can be a great accent colour for work.
- Wear green when you want to feel grounded and connected to nature.
- Wear green serpentine gemstones to support you in transition and being true to yourself.

Red

Powerful | passionate | exciting

Red is a very energetic colour. When you wear red, you will most certainly be noticed. While red is perceived as being a sexual colour, studies have shown that a subtle pop of red is more suggestive than an all-out red outfit. You can also use pops of red around your house in areas where you want to boost the energy.

Tips for wearing red

- Wear red from top to toe if you want to stand out.
- Wear with black or white for business.
- Choose a red that works with your skin tone (ask for help with this at your favourite makeup counter).
- Wear a red dress for a classic, feminine look.
- Wear a pop of red in accessories if all-out red feels too much for you.
- Wear red ruby gemstones when you want to overcome fears and obstacles and accomplish big goals.

Yellow

Creative | happy | adventurous

Yellow increases the production of serotonin in the brain and improves the mood of everyone around you when you wear it. People who wear yellow are seen as happy, optimistic and adventurous. They are often very creative people who are ready to explore and conquer the next opportunity. Yellow flowers on your desk or around your house are great for getting inspired.

Tips for wearing yellow

- Wear it when you or people around you need cheering up.
- Wear yellow stripes if solid yellow is too much for you.
- Wear it solid on the bottom with more subtle prints on top.
- Wear it as an accent colour in accessories.
- Wear it in winter to add a bit of sunshine to dark days.
- Wear yellow sapphire gemstones to turbocharge your vitality and sustain your vision when your energy is low.

Purple

Creative | insightful | sophisticated

Purple is rare in nature and expensive to create, which means that throughout history it has been associated with royalty and the privileged in society. It is also associated with supernatural powers (good to know, yes?). Light purples are light-hearted and romantic, while darker shades are more intellectual. Wearing purple helps to boost creativity and imagination, but too much of it can create moodiness. It is very useful when calming confrontational situations and also helps to create energy around learning new things.

Tips for wearing purple

- Purple makes every eye colour pop, so wear it close to your face when you want to connect with people.
- Wear it as a pop of colour with black or grey if you are not sure about wearing a full outfit in it.
- Some would say you shouldn't mix purple with other colours, but red and purple make a dramatic combination that work well in colour blocking.
- Consider purple as an accent colour with neutrals like taupes, silvers, metallic whites, bronze and pewters.

- Lavender, paler shades of purple and light lavender greys are amazing with blonde or grey hair.
- Wear purple rhodonite gemstones when you want to get clarity on your goals and unique gifts.

Pink

Feminine | calm | warm

Traditionally, pink has been seen as quite girly, flirty and uber-feminine. For this reason, it is often shunned by people who want to be taken seriously. However, pale pinks are calm, warm and non-aggressive and, when worn with black, can be quite edgy. Pink represents affection, friendship, approachability and harmony.

Tips for wearing pink

- Wear pink to promote happiness in those around you.
- Wear hot pink to communicate playfulness.
- Wear light pink to communicate tenderness.
- Pale pink is a great colour to wear when you want to wind down at night or to sleep in. Cosy pale pink blankets will have the same effect on everybody in your household.

- Wear pink gemstones for serenity, relaxation, contentment and to soften frustration.

Orange

Fun | cheerful | creative

Orange is a playful colour that promotes learning and energy. It is a mix of red and yellow, so it is also a mixture of those colour personalities. Use orange if you want to feel young and carefree. It can be a little too bright and overpowering, so use it in moderation, especially in tense situations.

Tips for wearing orange

- Add it as an accent colour to neutrals across the spectrum, from blacks to beiges and whites.
- If you are feeling brave, wear it with purple.
- If bright orange feels like too much, consider more peachy tones or add some playful orange accessories for summer.
- Give orange a try, the right tone for your skin will make it glow.
- Be careful of wearing with black, you don't want to look like Halloween!

- Wear orange topaz or sunstone gemstones to encourage growth and when you want to go after the things that empower you.

Neutrals

Classy | timeless | confident

Neutrals are colours that can go with anything. These are essential for building every woman's wardrobe. Choosing a whole wardrobe of neutrals may seem boring. However, doing so speaks of a woman's confidence, especially when iconic statement pieces mix and match, forming the building blocks of a timeless wardrobe. The key to the success of the neutrals wardrobe is to rejuvenate it each season, moving the look along to stay relevant.

Tips for wearing neutrals

- Invest in iconic statement pieces that can be worn in different ways.
- Inject a little bit of colour in the form of earthy pastels to keep it interesting.
- Use statement jewellery. Sunglasses show confidence and attitude if the rest of your outfit is neutral.
- Use statement shoes that align with your personality to create an edgy vibe to a neutral outfit.

- Use interesting accessories to dress existing outfits up for occasions.

A note on colours and workwear

It is worth mentioning some colour tips for work situations. When you want to just get on with things, fly under the radar and fade into the background, wear low contrast outfits. Colour combinations like browns, beiges and greens suggest that you would like to be left alone and give off a low energy, forgettable vibe. However, it's useful to know this for those days when you just want to get through that long to-do list!

You might not give off the vibe of setting the world on fire if you wear medium contrast outfits, such as a black skirt and a pale colour blouse, but you will be seen as being dependable and reliable. This combination is always a safe bet for work if you are uncertain about what is appropriate.

Wearing high contrast outfits say, for example, a dark skirt, a light top and a pop of colour in a scarf or accessories, all speak of confidence and being comfortable in positions of responsibility. It is the pop of brightness that does this. (Think of airline uniforms which often have a pop of red in their colour scheme.)

Easy ways to add colour to your wardrobe

- Choose a statement scarf.
- Wear a bright watch.
- A little colour goes a long way, so to just add just a subtle touch of colour, consider using layered bracelets and necklaces.
- Opt for a pop of colour in your lipstick.
- Add a bit of drama with big statement earrings.
- Add soft pastel versions of colour to your neutrals.
- Stick with one accent colour per outfit.
- Even if you don't want to wear colour, you can still get the benefit from using it in small leather accessories, like purses.
- Shoes are a great way to add colour, especially if you favour a lot of black in your wardrobe.

CHAPTER 11

Rock Your Body Type

Know your body to make the most of your assets

It's quite normal for everybody's weight to fluctuate all through life. Some situations make it difficult to control, especially if there are health issues and medication involved. We need to make the most of what we have at any given time and we need to stop beating ourselves up when we think we are less than perfect.

We are going to do a few things in this section.

We are going to find out:

1. What your body type is. There is no one perfect shape! Each one has its pros and cons, contrary to what you might currently believe.

2. What your assets are! Every shape has its assets. We will get focused on those, so that you will know how to empower yourself by highlighting your best bits and learning to stop obsessing over what you perceive to be your body flaws.
3. How to create an overall balance. Knowing how to visually balance the different areas of your body is the key to looking great, whatever shape you are.

The problem with body image

Body image is a big issue for a lot of people. Traditional fashion media and social media can paint unrealistic images of what body perfection looks like. It can be very depressing for us mere mortals who cannot help but compare ourselves and feel like we come up short.

The good news however, is that there is a growing trend on social media of health-conscious models and influencers promoting a more realistic and healthier attitude towards our bodies. It is great to see healthier well-toned bodies growing in popularity.

Your body shape changes throughout life. Don't let this knock you off course. Assess as it changes and let go of the past fast! Work with what you've got. Don't wait for it to change back. If it does it's a bonus! If it doesn't that is normal!

First of all, I want you to do two things.

1. Lose the weighing scales
2. Invest in a full-length mirror

Stepping on the weighing scales first thing in the morning is a terrible habit. If you are not happy with where the needle is pointed, it is never going to set you up for a good day. Why would you want to do that to yourself?

A full-length mirror to check your outfit for the day on the other hand, will show you if your overall look is balanced. You cannot judge how an outfit looks from checking out sections of it in a small mirror. It just does not work and if you do that, you will never be 100% confident that you are well put together. You need to see the overall look from head to toe. (I would however suggest and this comes from experience… If you are not happy with your weight, don't stand in front of the mirror until you are fully dressed!)

Body types

I have grouped the various body shapes into five main types and included some images and descriptions so you can get clarity on which one you are. I have also given some general guidelines on what to wear for each body shape, so you can accentuate your good bits and play down what you perceive to be your bad bits.

There are no hard and fast rules. Creating visual balance is the key to everything. There are just a few pointers to go with each body shape.

How to assess your body type

If you are having trouble identifying which shape you are. Get somebody to take a photo of you in your underwear, or you can take a selfie if you prefer. It is very often easier to see shapes in photos than in a mirror. You can even print it out and draw around your shape which will give you an even clearer picture of your shape. When you have identified your body shape, you can download the corresponding pdf from our website. If you save it to your phone, it can keep you focused when you go shopping.

https://marygrant.com/rock-your-body-shape/

Stepping on the weighing scales first thing in the morning is a terrible habit. If you are not happy with where the needle is pointed, it is never going to set you up for a good day. Why would you want to do that to yourself?

The Pear

Small bust | small waist | hips & thighs are wider than shoulders

This is also known as the triangle shape. If you are a pear, your top half will be narrow and you will have fuller hips and thighs. What you want to do is add volume to the top part of your body while wearing slimmer pieces on the bottom. This will create a visual balance between the two.

Looking great as a Pear

You probably have a very well defined shape and a great waist, so show it off! Use padded bras to give you extra fullness at the bust area. Boat necks, off the shoulders and wide scoop necklines will show off your defined and slim shoulders. Prints on the top half of your body, matched with a plain darker colour on the bottom, will also create balance with the dark colour visually reducing your hip size. Billowing tops nipped in at the waist will look fab on you and create fullness on your top half.

What to wear

- ✓ *Frills and flounces on sleeves*
- ✓ *Embellishments at the shoulders and neckline*
- ✓ *Light fullness in skirts and dresses*
- ✓ *Wide-leg pants in darker colours*
- ✓ *Wrap shirts and tops with a fitted waist*
- ✓ *A-line skirts*
- ✓ *Strapless dresses with full skirts*
- ✓ *Shrugs that close just under the bust*
- ✓ *Jackets with details*
- ✓ *High-neck shirts*
- ✓ *Structured coats with belt details at the waist*
- ✓ *Jeans with fading on the thigh area*

What to avoid

- ✓ *Cigarette pants*
- ✓ *Balloon dresses*
- ✓ *Mini skirts*
- ✓ *Bright colours on the lower half*
- ✓ *Bias cut skirts*

The Apple

Big bust | undefined waist | small hips| slim arms | slim legs

You may find that when you put on a bit of weight, it lands on your tummy area. Do not let it get into your head-space and drive you crazy. You can draw attention away from this and focus on your best assets. These are often your lovely slim legs and arms, so you want to highlight those by wearing fitted items there.

Looking great as an Apple

The first job is to get fitted for a good supportive bra, which will stop the girls from wandering. Use vertical lines to draw the eye down your body. This can be done with long necklaces, scarves worn long (not short), as well as vertical seams and details. Avoid horizontal lines which will chop you in two.

One of my favourite ways to dress this body shape is to use ruching diagonally across the middle section which draws the eye down. The ruching also creates wrinkles which visually reduce the size of any area where they appear.

What to wear

- ✓ *V-neck/scoop neck tops*
- ✓ *Shirts and T-shirt ruched in the middle*
- ✓ *Soft, textured fabrics*
- ✓ *A-line skirts and dresses*
- ✓ *Soft, flared trousers*
- ✓ *Tops that tie below the bust line*
- ✓ *Dresses that flow from under the bust line*
- ✓ *Tops that fall lower than the hip bone*
- ✓ *Jackets with well-defined shoulders*
- ✓ *Flat front trousers*
- ✓ *Ruched and draped tops with open necklines*
- ✓ *Tops that flare from under the bustline*
- ✓ *Straight front jackets and cardis (long straight lines that draw the eye down the body)*
- ✓ *Straight duster coats*
- ✓ *Any lines that draw the eye downwards*

What to avoid

- ✓ *Anything too fitted*
- ✓ *Rough textures*
- ✓ *Shapeless, boxy items*
- ✓ *Details near the waist*
- ✓ *Turtle or round necks*
- ✓ *Off the shoulder or boat necks*
- ✓ *Horizontal stripes*

The Column

Shoulder and hip width the same | slight waist | long legs

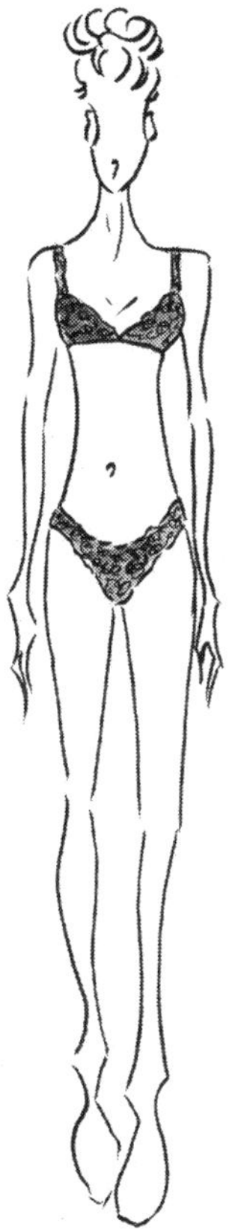

This body shape is also often described as the racehorse of the group. You have long limbs, are statuesque and are probably quite tall. You may have been teased for having a body like a boy as a teenager. That was stressful then, but you can really rock this body shape now as you can wear almost anything!

Looking great as a Column

The Column shape body does have curves, but these are stretched out over your length. You can use volume to create curves anywhere you want them, so there are a lot of opportunities for you to play around with different looks and very few restrictions. The main thing to be conscious of are long fitted lines which will make you appear taller.

What to wear

- ✓ *Different blocks of colour on the top and bottom to break up your long frame*
- ✓ *Flared trousers*
- ✓ *A-line skirts*
- ✓ *Single button jackets*
- ✓ *Bias cut dresses*
- ✓ *¾ length belted coats*
- ✓ *Cropped trousers*
- ✓ *Round-necked jumpers*
- ✓ *Gathered shirts*
- ✓ *Belted tube tops*
- ✓ *Wide belts in darker colours*
- ✓ *Boat necks*
- ✓ *Off the shoulder tops*
- ✓ *Flowing and billowing tops, belted*
- ✓ *Embellishments at bust and shoulders*
- ✓ *Structured shoulder jackets*

What to avoid

- ✓ *Straight dresses in one colour*
- ✓ *Boxy jackets*
- ✓ *Cropped tops*
- ✓ *Dropped waists*

The Cornet

Broad shoulders | small boobs | undefined waist | slim hips | long legs

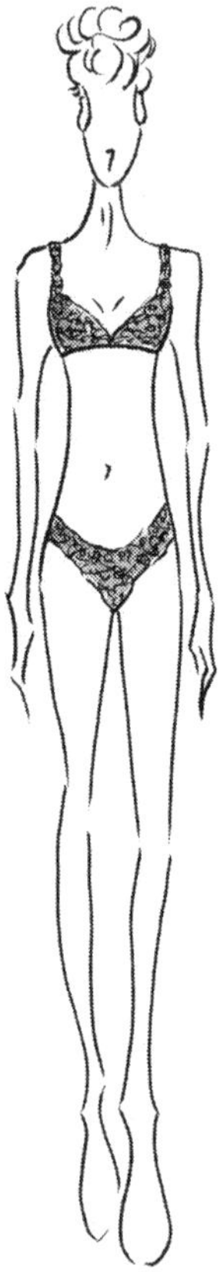

You have strong shoulders and a slim body. You are the perfect clothes hanger and while you may sometimes long for curves, you have the body of a supermodel. You can wear anything and look fabulous! For you, the art is about creating curves where they may be absent and knowing the very few things you should try to avoid.

Looking great as a cornet

Asymmetrical lines in soft floating fabrics will look ethereal and fabulous on you, as will any cuts which create curves around the body. Soft ruching and diagonal tucks and folds can be belted in interesting ways. Patterns that vary in size and shape will also create the impression of curves. Slashed and asymmetrical necklines will look great on you reducing the width of your shoulders and create balance with your slim hips.

What to wear

- ✓ *Long or short sleeves*
- ✓ *Wide shoulder straps*
- ✓ *Ruffles on your upper body*
- ✓ *Draping and gathers*
- ✓ *Anything that exaggerates your hips*
- ✓ *Fitted shoulders*
- ✓ *A-line dresses and skirts*
- ✓ *Long dresses*
- ✓ *Angled pockets*
- ✓ *Asymmetrical panelling*

What to avoid

- ✓ *¾ length sleeves*
- ✓ *Baggy, shapeless dresses*
- ✓ *Spaghetti straps*
- ✓ *Deeply scooped necklines*
- ✓ *Masculine cuts when you want to be more feminine*

The Hourglass

Generous bust | small waist | generous hips and thighs

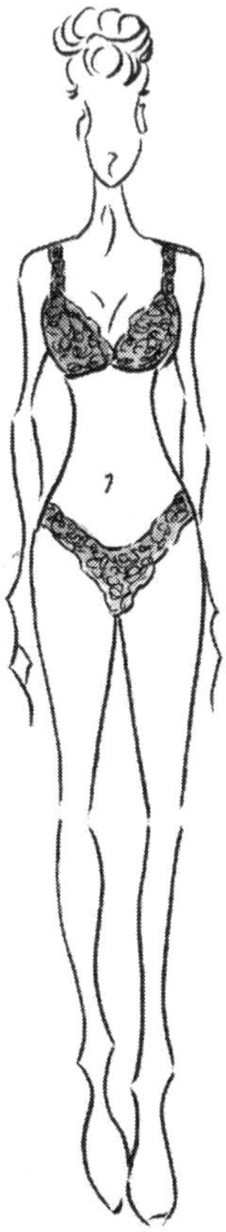

This is the most classically feminine body type, you are a goddess! This is also seen as the sexiest body type. If you have it, lucky you, embrace it! Your bust and hip lines are well balanced. Your waist is defined and you are in proportion.

Looking great as an Hourglass

The key to dressing this most feminine body type is to keep the top and bottom of your body in proportion while accentuating your waist. Simple lines with a well-defined waist will look great on you. Adding belts to flowing and simple tops will allow you to add light volume and femininity without losing your shape. The trick to wearing anything floaty and romantic is to keep it transparent and wear something that is fitted underneath so that you can still clearly see the outline of your body.

What to wear

- ✓ *A well fitted, supportive bra*
- ✓ *Simple lines with a well-defined waist*
- ✓ *Wrap, fitted or belted tops and dresses*
- ✓ *Add a belt to simple basic and flowing tops*
- ✓ *Tailored shirts and jackets that nip in at the waist*
- ✓ *Deep V and scoop necklines*
- ✓ *Draped flowing trousers*
- ✓ *Open necklines*
- ✓ *Slim body-con skirts*

What to avoid

- ✓ *Frilly shirts*
- ✓ *Big bows*
- ✓ *Lots of volume*
- ✓ *Chunky knits*
- ✓ *High necklines*
- ✓ *Baggy clothes*

A note on height

Height is something that crops up time and time again, no matter what body shape people have. I come across so many women who just want to be a few inches taller but don't want to wear heels. There's a huge choice on the market of platform/wedge shoes that will give you the height you desire while still allowing you to run around.

A favourite tip though, especially for people with short legs, is nude heels that match your skin tone add several inches to the length of your legs!

Section 3 Summary

I hope you had fun with this section. You now know your style type, your dominant colour group and your body shape, as well as why we make mistakes and why what you wear matters.

We are going to take all this on board and move into the next section where you will start to decide what your wardrobe building formula will look like.

SECTION 4

Choose Your 'a la carte' Wardrobe Formula

"Learn the rules like a pro,
so you can break them like an artist."

-PABLO PICASSO-

Introduction to Section 4

In this section, I am going to explore a few different types of wardrobe. Although there is crossover between all of them, each type has its signature personality and you will identify with some of them more than others. You may lean towards one type or choose the combined elements of several, but whichever type of wardrobe you choose, there are no hard and fast rules. I just want to give you a few guidelines to help you to make more informed choices.

I will give you the signature character of each at the start of each chapter. You can then have some fun creating your individual wardrobe by using elements of the ones that speak to you. As you go through the different stages in life, your needs will change, as will your signature style. Revisit the different sections for inspiration as you evolve your style.

I combine elements of all of these wardrobe types when I am designing our collections, ensuring that they are timeless. You never know which ones I am going to use from season to season, which keeps people guessing and gets them excited to see what is coming next. You can steal my strategy and use it to be timeless, so that you will never become boring or predictable.

For all of the different wardrobe styles available, keep in mind that you will be dressing for your own personality, that is a given. Whichever wardrobe type you choose, you will start from a place of knowing what works for you. As your confidence grows in your own choices, you will care less about what people think, which is very empowering. If you are not 100% convinced of that yet, trust the process, keep an open mind and do the work.

This section does not cover "how to" create each wardrobe type as, at this point, I just want to give you the knowledge. I will cover everything that you need to know about creating your wardrobe in a later chapter.

CHAPTER 12

The Timeless Wardrobe

Wardrobe style signature
Pieces that do not date. They will look as good in 10 years' time as they did on the day you bought them.

What is a timeless wardrobe?

There are some disagreements about what exactly a timeless wardrobe is. Some sources suggest that you only have a timeless wardrobe if you work with a specific list of pieces. I would disagree. Working to a list is great for people who are not interested in being individual. But you didn't come here for that.

My belief of what makes a wardrobe timeless comes directly from working with my customers for the last two and a half decades. There are certain pieces from my earliest collections that customers still brag about wearing today. Their daughters often come to buy their first pieces from our collections after raiding their mothers' wardrobes and borrowing these pieces. When garments can be worn for decades and then passed on to another generation, that is what I call 'timeless', and is different from the typical timeless checklist, which includes items like trench coats and pencils skirts.

Being timeless does not mean buying boring forgettable pieces, that's not the point. The point is that they are not so bang on-trend they will look wrong in 6 months' time. If you have an emotional reaction to something on the day you buy it, whether you fell in love with the details or just felt amazing when you put it on, you will continue having this response every time you wear that item for years to come, especially if you keep reinventing it. Creating your own timeless wardrobe in this way is very inspiring and gives you great confidence in your own style. This, in turn, makes you more confident in every other area of your life.

It is best to focus on flattering cuts and create go-to outfits where less is more as they will make you look effortlessly put together. The trick is to find pieces that are a little bit unusual – either in the cut or the details. Also, mix your statement pieces with simpler well-cut, quality pieces and invest in outerwear. These pieces may be at the upper end of your budget, but you will get so much wear out of them over many years, the cost per wear over time will be very little. Over time, you will also have a collection of pieces that are unique to you, creating serious wardrobe envy. What woman doesn't want to know that her wardrobe cannot be exactly replicated by anybody else?

You cannot do this with cheap fabrics or badly made clothes. Even though you will have to invest a bit more in these pieces, you will be well rewarded by the empowerment and value the piece offers over the course of its lifetime. Add elements of trends if you want to be relevant to the moment, but this type of wardrobe building will save you a fortune over time.

Any pieces that evoke feelings of rarity, excitement, curiosity and emotion are key to this wardrobe. Be forward-focused rather than delving into the past. Getting stuck in a specific era will kill this wardrobe. You don't want people to be able to put a timestamp on you. Evolve by constantly looking for interesting angles which you can pick up from fashion trends and add in.

You may need to transition into building your timeless wardrobe. Start with analysing what you have already. You won't be getting rid of anything that is very current or trend-driven straight away. They can be edited out over a couple of seasons. Alternatively, you can sell them on while they still have value to somebody else and build up your funds for some new timeless pieces.

When you develop a timeless wardrobe, you should have no interest in quick fixes as you will be buying less and only buying the things that you really love. You will be able to justify that handbag you have had your eye on for ages, or you will be able to buy that fabulous coat because you know it will be brought out for not years, but decades.

If you do this, you will be rewarded by that great feeling of still loving your timeless pieces 10 or even 20 years from now.

"

I have a raincoat that is 19 years old. Every time I wear it, people still compliment me. I still have all my pinnies from over the years, my daughters are wearing them now!"

"

-HELEN MARTIN-
Stylist

What are the benefits of a timeless wardrobe?

- Over time, you will end up with a wardrobe that cannot be replicated by somebody else.
- The wardrobe's unique pieces will remind you that you are worth investing in every time you wear them.
- Everything you have works all the time.

- You will buy better quality and buy less.
- You will be able to afford the things you really want.
- You will make faster decisions and shop earlier, ensuring that you don't miss out on your size in those limited pieces.

Key pieces of a timeless wardrobe:

- Limited editions from your favourite collections. You must shop early for these!
- Simple tops and bottoms in good quality fabrics that can be mixed and matched to create different outfits.
- Iconic dresses, skirts and tops. Look for the unusual details and great cuts.
- Statement coats and jackets. These will come out year after year, don't be afraid to make them fun and interesting!
- Bold statement jewellery. These pieces can be the focal point of several different simple outfits.
- Good quality shoes with good support. Your feet will thank you for looking after them!
- Investment handbags which make you feel like you are worth investing in. Resist buying lots of cheaper

bags as they cannot compete with a handful of carefully chosen good bags acquired over time.

- Contrasting textures. Use them to add interest to simple outfits.
- Versatile accessories like belts and scarves that you can play around with and wear in different ways.

Top tips for building a timeless wardrobe:

- Shop early in the season so that you have the choice of the best pieces. We see so many people waltzing in our doors weeks after a style has sold out who end up being so disappointed that they missed the one thing they wanted.
- Get friendly with store stylists so they will call you when the best new pieces come in.
- Experiment with your style. Take one thing into the dressing room that you wouldn't normally try. It could be the very thing that will influence your style and rejuvenate several pieces that you already have.
- Always be on the lookout for interesting pieces. Whenever you travel to new places, check out the local style and see if any treasures fit in with your existing wardrobe (don't get carried away though, stay true to your style so a moment of madness

doesn't result in purchasing things that look silly when you get home).

- Only buy things that work with what you already have, or that move you in a new direction.
- Do not buy cheap fabrics or badly made clothes. Even though you will have to invest a bit more in these pieces, you will be well rewarded in the empowerment and value you will receive over the lifetime of the piece.
- Plan a trip to a makeup counter that employs makeup artists at the start of every season. This will keep your makeup bang up to date. Likewise with your hair. Keep it bang up to date and when the greys outnumber your original colour, go lighter as your skin tone is also changing and dark hair can be very harsh.

CHAPTER 13

The Lifestyle Wardrobe

Wardrobe style signature
Groups of outfits created by strategically planning around the wearer's everyday life.

What is the lifestyle wardrobe?

I have heard people say, "everybody has a lifestyle wardrobe" and yes, that is true. However, not everybody has a strategically planned lifestyle wardrobe. Buying clothes for the fun stuff is a great reason to go shopping, but if you are not careful, you can end up having a very unbalanced wardrobe. You might have lots of things that you bought for occasions or going out but you will find that the section of your wardrobe dedicated to every day is lacking and uninspiring. What you want to do is make sure that you have a balanced wardrobe for your everyday needs.

People with really busy lives really benefit from this type of wardrobe. Whether you are running your own business and wearing a lot of different hats, travelling a lot or even raising a young family, there will be lots of boxes that you need to tick so that you are covered for every eventuality. I clearly remember the day when I found myself loading three small kids into the car as a newly single mum and thought to myself, my wardrobe needs to change. It needed to become more practical and easy-care. This was when I introduced jerseys to our collection, so I could still be dressed nicely but have the freedom to move in a way that a physical lifestyle demands. I knew if I had that problem, other people would too.

When your life is chaotic and you are meeting yourself coming back, it is very easy to get stuck in a rut. Your personal identity can disappear very quickly when you throw on jeans and a hoody every day. Everybody else's needs become more important, especially when you are raising a young family. It is very easy to lose yourself without even realising it is happening when you are catering to everybody else's needs first.

In my research, I came across an article on 'unclothed cognition', which is a scientific study into how clothes can influence how a person feels. One study reported in ***The Journal of Experimental Social Psychology*** found that the attention of people who were asked to wear a white coat increased when they were told it was a doctor's lab coat. Interestingly, the coat didn't have the same effect when they were told it was a painter's coat.

This is relevant to what we wear every day because the clothes we wear influence how we are perceived by the world and that, in turn, affects how we feel about ourselves. So, it is very important not to become invisible in the way that we dress every day. Paying more attention to how you dress every day influences how you feel about everything in a positive way. When you feel good, you have more energy and everybody around you benefits from that.

So, it is well worth assessing your wardrobe and seeing if it has a positive influence on you every day, whatever it is you spend most of your day doing.

> "*I have a new motto inspired by Bronagh, my stylist, who said we should never save our best looks for good wear, we should rock them and inspire ourselves every day!*"
>
> -OBI JAMES-
> Leadership coach

What are the benefits of a lifestyle wardrobe?

- Putting the time into your initial planning will result in you not having to think as much about outfits later. You will be able to jump up and go every morning.
- You will never be under pressure to have something to wear, everything will just work for your real life.
- You will spend less time shopping and have more time for everything else.
- You will make fewer wasteful purchases.
- Taking the time to assess exactly where your time is being spent in the planning of your wardrobe is usually a big eye-opener. Most people start to have 'aha' moments about where all their precious time is going. This is a big added non-wardrobe bonus as, when you are aware, you will start to look for ways to help you save and create time in all other areas of your life.

Key pieces in a lifestyle wardrobe:

- Easy-care, time-saving fabrics that can be steamed rather than ironed.
- Versatile mix and match separates, which can be used to create different outfits.

- Knitwear for travelling and hopping in and out of the car.
- Jeans. Invest in decent jeans if you wear them a lot. They hold their shape better and you will feel better wearing them. Don't blow your budget on an outfit for an occasion and then buy cheap jeans. This is a mistake we see all the time that does nothing for your self-esteem as it is what you wear every day that matters.
- Comfy shoes. Beware of wearing flat shoes with no support every day as you will be heading for trouble with your feet down the road. They are fine occasionally. These include shoes like flat pumps, flip-flops, you get the idea.
- Cross body bags are a lifesaver when you are on the go all the time. They keep your hands free and reduce the backache that is induced by carrying handbags which get fuller the busier your life is! This leaves you with more energy at the end of the day.
- Capsules of mix and match Jerseys give you endless choices and ease of movement.
- Flick back to the colour section to make sure that you have some of the mood-enhancing colours for those more challenging days.

Top tips for building a lifestyle wardrobe:

- Have a shopping list of the gaps in your wardrobe handy on your phone so that you can take advantage of an unexpected half-hour here or there to shop.
- If you can, shop once a season for your main pieces and add interesting pieces when you stumble across them. You will spend less if you shop this way. It's also a great way to shop for kids and reduces the time you would otherwise spend shopping.
- No matter how casual your wardrobe is, have a few pieces that inspire you that you can pull out when you get a little bit of time for yourself. Nothing will give you a burst of energy and renewed vitality faster than wearing something a little bit special.
- Be open to trying new things to keep your wardrobe interesting. A great place to start looking for interesting ideas is on the archetype shopping lists that aren't your own.
- Buy pieces that travel well and are easy-care. You won't need special shopping trips for holidays, etc. and life will be less stressful when you can just throw a few things in a bag and go.

CHAPTER 14

Ageless Dressing

Wardrobe style signature
Clothes are chosen for the personality of the wearer that are individual and subtly camouflage the elements of the body that the wearer does not want to highlight, making it hard to put an age on her.

What is the ageless wardrobe?

This is a wardrobe-building strategy that may interest you most if you are of "a certain age". That expression irritates me a little, what does it even mean? It's like ageing can only be spoken of in whispers.

Now that I am on the 'wrong' side of 50, I can absolutely confirm that something magical happens when you cross that threshold. You know without a doubt that you have earned the right to not give a hoot (I normally use a different word that is not very polite in print) what anybody else thinks of you! You will not, up to this point, have experienced the freedom and confidence that this brings!

The wisdom that comes with age is a gift to be celebrated and should win hands-down over wanting to look younger. Take what is authentically yours and rock it!

At some stage in your 50s, it is likely you'll have finished raising your kids. While this can be a bit traumatic in itself, move on fast, because the most exciting times – if you choose them – are right ahead. There is so much time to explore all the things you have put on hold while raising and educating a family. It is quite possible that you still have another lifetime ahead of you and it is so exciting to know that you get to decide what it will look like. Looking forward, experimenting with new things, learning, creating, starting a new job after raising a family, or even a business, will all keep you relevant and evolving.

Do not allow yourself to slip into middle age and granny shoes! Let your wardrobe reflect your personality and the power you have earned. Try new things and don't worry about any body parts which may be heading south. Concentrate on being healthy instead of looking younger. You will have more energy and this is contagious, as energy breeds energy. Keep looking for those gorgeous timeless pieces that excite you and have some fun with them.

The wisdom that comes with age is a gift to be celebrated and should win hands-down over wanting to look younger. Take what is authentically yours and rock it!

Camouflage the things that you don't want to draw attention to and keep assessing your body type as it naturally changes.

Choose pieces that do not put you into any age bracket that people can identify. You could be 40 or you could be 70. You know and observe the rules that make sense so that you never look like mutton dressed as lamb, but you never conform to society's perceptions of age either.

"

I don't want to dress like my daughter and I don't want to dress like my mother. My body shape has changed and I choose pieces that allow me to not focus on that fact. I work with the body shape that I have, and pay attention to my assets. Confidence and wellbeing are the accessories I wear every day.

"

-BRID FALLON-
Hotelier

What are the benefits of an ageless wardrobe?

- You will always leave people wondering what age you actually are!
- You will become immune to society's expectations

- You will grow the confidence needed to stand out from the crowd
- You will always be relevant, always be planning for the future and never living in the past!
- You will literally rock till you drop!

Key pieces of an ageless wardrobe:

- Depending on your body shape, combine skinny on top and loose on the bottom or vice versa.
- Strategic sleeve and skirt lengths to cover the elbows and knees
- Layered lengths that mix & match
- Asymmetricals
- Sheer tops for under deep necklines and sleeveless dresses
- Unstructured pieces
- Good everyday underwear and shapewear
- Invest in footwear
- Long neckpieces and pendants to draw the eye downwards

- Short neckpieces to bring attention to your face (but not chokers which draw attention to your neck, unless you have a great neck)
- Soft chiffon scarves in pastel shades to reflect light up to your face

Top tips for building an ageless wardrobe:

- If you haven't done so already, get to know some stylists, either by booking private sessions or going into stores with staff of a similar age. They will have seen lots of people go through this stage and will have a tool kit of tricks to deal with all the things that could invade your headspace should you let them!
- Choose pieces that do not put you into any age bracket that people can identify. You could be 40 or you could be 70. You know and observe the rules that make sense so that you will never look like mutton dressed as lamb, but you never conform to society's perceptions of age either.
- Do not live in the past, accept changes to your body gracefully and move on fast!
- Choose things that you have an emotional response to and make you feel fabulous!

- Update your hair and makeup as you move from decade to decade. Our skin tones change over time and sticking to what you did in your 20s and 30s, won't work when you are in your 40s & 50s.
- Everything starts to sag a little when we get older. So what? Just camouflage what you don't want to draw attention to! (Or learn to walk on your hands.)
- Wear light layers when you start having hot flashes, so you can whip something off and then pop it back on afterwards. Some people can feel a little chilly afterwards, so a nice soft wrap will be like a little hug.

CHAPTER 15

The Secret of Layering

Wardrobe style signature
A versatile wardrobe of individual pieces that can be mixed & matched and worn in combinations of layers.

What is the layered wardrobe?

Layering has been around for centuries. From cavewomen in their animal skins right through the different periods in history where dresses were layered over corsets. Thankfully the modern-day version of layering is a lot more practical and comfortable.

Layering is useful in all climates. In colder climates, 2 thin layers create more heat than 1 heavier layer as air is trapped between them. They are also useful for absorbing sweat and protecting against rain and wind. In warmer climates, light outer layers over inner base layers protect the body from the ultraviolet rays of the sun.

Sports brands use layering a lot by as they have technical aspects for different fabrics, which have different uses. These range from fitted base layers for performance to layers for warmth to outer shell layers for protection.

In fashion, for everyday wear, we are well used to layering up outfits, especially for casual wear. We all know how to take a pair of jeans and a shirt and add various layers, including sweaters, jackets, scarves, etc.

There is another aspect of layering that is less common, which is an art form that we have perfected as a brand over the last 10-15 years. We take base layers of our jerseys, which are all designed to mix and match as outfits for every day, and add one key piece that transforms them into an outfit for a special occasion. We have completely changed how people shop by doing this one simple thing. The system works for every kind of occasion and several brides have even created their wedding day outfit this way. On top of the base layer, you add one feature piece, be it a lace or voile dress or a chiffon tunic. The beauty of this system is that all of the pieces can be worn in several different ways. Both casual outfits and outfits for several occasions can be created just by swopping different pieces.

About 70% of our customers come back season after season to update their wardrobe and one new piece can

Layering is useful in all climates. In colder climates, 2 thin layers create more heat than 1 heavier layer. In warmer climates, light outer layers over inner base layers protect the body from the ultraviolet rays rejuvenate several outfits. This saves them a fortune over time and they end up creating capsule wardrobes that are unique to them.

If you would like to know more about how to do this, our stylists are always putting new combinations together which we post on social media, so have a look at our Facebook or Instagram pages for some inspiration.

There is one particular time in life when this wardrobe strategy can be a lifesaver. We have been told by customers that their body temperature goes all over the place when they go through the menopause, so lighter layers can help. They can be added and removed during the day, which removes a lot of the discomfort that goes with it.

What are the benefits of a layered wardrobe?

- Your favourite pieces become timeless and seasonless as you can keep reinventing them and layering them with other pieces.
- Your wardrobe will be refreshed with just a few new pieces which mix in with existing pieces.
- When it comes to occasions, you will always have something to wear with a layering capsule as you can create different combinations of pieces.
- It is great for travelling as you can add and remove layers when you go in and out of air conditioning.

Plus, you can create a capsule of pieces which will mix and match and take up very little room in a suitcase.

- This is a natural choice for those with a creative style, so you will always be inspired by yourself!
- Layering is a great way to introduce colour and textures.

Key pieces of a layered wardrobe:

- Fitted jersey basics
- Skinny jeans
- Good quality leggings
- Chiffons and voiles
- Lightweight fabrics
- Cardis
- Belts
- Lace for occasions
- Alternative colours in base layers
- Layered jewellery
- Coats and cropped jackets
- Long cardis

- Faux fur gilet
- Sleeveless pieces and various sleeve lengths to be worn layered together
- Close-fitting base layers

Top tips for building a layered wardrobe:

- Buy the best jerseys that you can find.
- Buy good quality fitted jeans.
- Experiment with dresses over jeans and different textures.
- Use belts to tie layers together and nip in at the waist.
- Wrap tops are great worn over sheer layers.
- Don't be afraid to mix prints.
- Only use one or 2 colour families or your outfit can look too broken up.
- Layer necklaces.
- Make sure that 2 or more necklines worn together complement each other, rather than fight for attention.
- Use lighter layers to avoid adding bulk. Use only one bulky item in an outfit.

- Use vertical lines to add height.
- Use accessories to pull outfits together.
- Shop when you are not under pressure to buy for an occasion.
- Don't have more than 2 colours unless they are in a print.

"

I started with a few basic jersey pieces. Each season I add one or two pieces to my collection. Because I can mix and match the colours, my outfit choices multiply each time!

"

-CLAIRE GOLDEN-
Stylist

CHAPTER 16

The Capsule Wardrobe

Wardrobe style signature
A minimal wardrobe of pieces chosen to mix and match together and where less frivolous and more mindful options are prioritised.

What is the capsule wardrobe?

There has been a lot of talk in recent years about capsule wardrobes, but it is not a new concept. The phrase capsule wardrobe was coined by Susie Faux, the owner of a London boutique called Wardrobe back in the 1970s.

The main principle of a capsule wardrobe is that you live with fewer clothes. You declutter your life which declutters your head.

The main principle of a capsule wardrobe is that you live with fewer clothes. You declutter your life which declutters your head.

A very easy way to test if this is likely to work for you is to clear your desk or the worktops in your kitchen. In either case, just put back the things that you need. If it is your desk, put back only a candle or a vase of flowers, a notebook, a nice pen and maybe your laptop, that's it. If it is your kitchen worktops, put back only your kettle and again, a candle or a vase of flowers. How do you feel afterwards? Do you feel anxious, wanting to fill the space up again immediately or do you feel inspired by all the space? If you feel anxious maybe this is not the best wardrobe strategy for you. If you feel inspired, you'll find that applying this principle to your wardrobe will give you the same feeling every day.

This is my chosen wardrobe strategy and I can confirm that living with fewer clothes makes me feel that my head is less cluttered. I kinda joke that I like to keep my head empty, but it's not really a joke. When my head is clear, it leaves lots of space for the good stuff to happen, like getting inspired, being mindful, enjoying the simple pleasures and learning, lots and lots of learning.

As I was reading lots of different articles online to see what everybody else was saying about capsule wardrobes, I found myself rolling my eyes. Many people said they had tried the concept and failed. And no wonder! Whatever type of wardrobe strategy you follow it should be fun and yet here were all these people trying to follow rules about how many pieces you can have and what those pieces should be. How boring and uninspiring?!

So, here's the thing, having a capsule wardrobe is a great idea. Take the principles and ditch the rules! Or even better still, make up your own. And guess what, those rules can change, as many times as you want them to!

The rules that you want to ditch are #1 you need to have a set number of items and #2 there is a set list of what these items need to be.

Your rules state that you can have as many items as you want, within reason, and they can be whatever you want them to be. The trick is to make sure that you have lots of combinations of outfits, using each piece that you have. If an item only works in one specific way, it's not going to be a great choice for this type of wardrobe strategy. Your individual pieces can be basic pieces in neutral colours that all mix and match, or jaw-dropping, show-stopping pieces that mix with simpler pieces in different ways. My capsule signature is pinnies, dungarees, oversized shirts, jeans, jackets and coats. These are complemented by simple jersey pieces that are essential for changing things up and for days when I am flat out doing all the physical stuff. For some people, jewellery and accessories will be an essential part of their capsule. For me, if I remember to put on a watch, I am doing well. The choice is yours.

Be true to your style. Don't be pressurised by other people into wearing what they think you should wear. If you feel resistance, stay confident in the fact that people are getting the best version of you when you are true to yourself, they will soon get the message. If they need reminding, gently remind them and then do your thing!

> "*I have built up my wardrobe over many years. I never get rid of my pieces; I still love them all. Each season, I add new pieces from the collection. Every new purchase not only moves my wardrobe on, it creates several new outfit options which are unique to me.*"
>
> -MARY MASTERSON-
> Publican

What are the benefits of a capsule wardrobe?

- You will become very mindful of what you are buying. You will be less attracted to the quick hits and more frivolous purchases that don't serve you well.
- You will enjoy the clear space physically and mentally so everything has to earn its place in your wardrobe. You will have more time for all the important

things like following your big life dreams when you have a clearer head.

- Day to evening and special occasions can be achieved just by changing accessories, jewellery and shoes.
- Shopping will not be a hobby, so you will have time for a real, fulfilling hobby that feeds your soul and calms your mind.
- When you shop less, you buy more of the things you really love, the things that light you up.
- You will become a master at creating different options with fewer things, a skill which spills into the rest of your life.
- It is great for apartment living and travelling lifestyles.
- Being mindful when you are shopping is a great contribution towards sustainability.
- Clutter takes energy, so when you eliminate it, you will have more!

Key pieces of a capsule wardrobe:

While I'm not going to tell you what to wear, we do need a rough checklist so that we don't forget the basics like our knickers! I do this all the time when travelling! So make your own substitutes here.

- Your signature pieces, aka your show-stoppers or the things that you will become known for
- Pants
- Skirts
- Dresses
- Jeans
- T-shirts
- Shirts
- Jackets
- Cardis & knitwear
- Shoes that transform outfits from casual to dressy
- Interesting jewellery
- Accessories

Top tips for building a capsule wardrobe:

- Know what you are missing before you go shopping.
- Always be on the lookout for a fabulous addition to your wardrobe rather than being under pressure coming up to an occasion.
- Be true to your style whatever the occasion.
- A simple change of shoes or accessories can take you from day to evening or a more special event. Do not feel pressured by others, you will get better at this the more you practise.
- Stay focused!
- Buy iconic pieces that you will get lots of wear out of.
- Buy pieces that you can dress up or dress down by changing shoes and accessories.
- Save embellishments for coats, scarves, etc. that finish off simpler outfits.

CHAPTER 17

About Occasions

This is a bonus chapter which doesn't strictly come under wardrobe types, but instead highlights where a lot of waste occurs. I want you to keep this in mind before we move into the next section.

No matter what your preferred wardrobe style is, you will get invited to occasions. Outfits for occasions should not take up the biggest part of your wardrobe investment. I won't tell you to allocate 1/365th of your clothing budget to that one wedding you have to attend in the year, but you get the idea!

There are ways of shopping for an occasion that will ensure you get lots of wear out of your purchases.

The problem with occasions

I have touched on this in a few different places but I think it is worthy of a mention all of its own as we see people spending way too much money on outfits for special occasions, at the expense of a wardrobe which will make them feel great every day.

Shopping trips prompted by an upcoming special occasion can be a great kickstart to getting your wardrobe into shape or evolving your look with key new pieces.

There are two types of people that we see in our stores most commonly. There are those who love getting dressed up for special occasions and have a wardrobe of dresses they get lots of wear from as they also have very busy social lives. This is great. Job done.

Then there are those for whom dressy social engagements do not come around very often. In this case, shopping for occasions can be wasteful, stressful, exhausting and just plain expensive. Every day, we see people coming through our doors who have walked the legs off themselves looking for an outfit for a wedding. They really don't want to spend their clothing budget on things that they won't get the wear out of. If they have not developed their personal style or if they allow other people to dictate to them, they can feel under pressure to dress in a certain way. They are uninspired, overwhelmed and often in need of a Xanax by the time we get our hands on them!

There are ways of shopping for an occasion that will ensure you get lots of wear out of your purchases

If you are shopping for a special occasion, unless you are a member of a wedding party, do not spend a fortune on things that will sit in your wardrobe never to be seen again.

The benefits of mindful shopping for an occasion

- While an occasion is a great excuse to add some new pieces to your wardrobe, pay attention to your personal style and choose things that you can wear afterwards with pieces that you already have. If you are buying a whole new outfit, a few well-chosen pieces that mix and match and can be used to create several outfits are going to be a much better investment than one piece that is just what it is.
- Remember that a few pieces that evolve your existing wardrobe will ensure that you get loads of wear out of your clothes. You will feel great every time you wear them and get great value per wear over their lifetime.
- Buy mix and match pieces that can be dressed up or dressed down and you will end up with a whole capsule of pieces that can be worn for occasions in different ways.

- You might want to consider borrowing or renting for more formal occasions so you can save your money for your everyday investments.

Key pieces for an occasional wardrobe:

- A black dress that reflects your personal style.
- A killer classic pair of black heels will serve you well for many years and can transform lots of different outfits from day to occasion wear.
- Nude, metallic or crystal shoes and matching clutch work for summer occasions, with a whole range of colours and prints. These will ensure that you do not have to buy matching accessories every time.
- Statement necklaces dress up the simplest of outfits.
- Chiffon and tulle skirts add length to shorter dresses and transform them into an outfit for an occasion.
- Silk or cashmere wraps to cover your arms and complete outfits.
- Simple cuts in metallic tops that can be worn with various skirts or trousers.
- A couple of tailored jackets in great fabrics or with interesting details that mix with several things in your wardrobe. These will not only dress loads of

outfits up for an understated occasional look, but can also be worn every day over shirts and jeans.

- A few special outer layered pieces in chiffons, voiles and lace can transform the more basic pieces in your wardrobe.

Top tips for building an occasional wardrobe:

- Buy things that make you feel happy and confident and that are comfortable.
- Don't ask too many people for their input into what you wear. Get confident with your own choices and you won't need their opinions.
- Do not let other people dictate to you what you wear. Be firm. Tell them what they really want is your best version of yourself and they need to respect your choices.
- Do conform to general colour schemes if you are part of a wedding party.
- When it comes to weddings, keeping it simple will mean that you can get a lot of wear out of the same pieces. Only the wedding party should go all out.

Calculate what you will need

Just before we move on, here's a quick exercise to help you calculate your lifestyle so that you can plan your wardrobe to cover everything that you will need.

1. Make a list of all the things that you do in a typical week, including work, travelling, doing school runs, cooking, gym, socialising, sleeping.
2. Group together all the similar activities that you can wear the same clothes for.
3. Calculate the percentage of the week that each group represents.

Your budget for clothes should be allocated in proportion to the time that is spent on different groups of activities. Make a note of any special occasions that you have coming up in the next 6 months to make sure you have them covered.

For the purpose of calculating your clothing budget, you can minus off sleep if you want to. However, before you do this, I would like you to consider something.

If you are like most women I know, the only few minutes you might get for yourself during the whole day could be the last few minutes before you climb into bed. There is nothing like a nice shower, some body lotion and a nice pair of grown-up PJs (by that I mean lose the bunnies and love hearts) to finish off your day nicely and feel empowered. When you take that time for yourself, you may just find the following day gets off to a really great start!

With all of these things considered, use this information to make sure that you allocate your shopping budget in proportion to your needs.

Make a note of the gaps in your wardrobe so that you can stay focused on what you need rather than getting distracted by the things you won't get enough wear out of. The object of the game is to feel great every day, not just occasionally.

Section 4 Summary

Now you know all about the different wardrobe types and how you can adapt them to suit yourself. Mine combines elements of all five wardrobe types. So, I'll always aim for timeless and ageless and don't buy anything that won't get worn all the time (lifestyle). Most of my outfits will have two layers on my top half, as I like to build on a jersey vest, and everything I have works together (capsule). I am covered for occasionwear outfits which for me, are always understated which I complete with sparkly jewellery to dress my outfit up.

Keep it simple to start with. You can draw on the different influences as you become more confident in your choices.

Remember the wardrobe types are guidelines, not rules. There ARE no rules!

SECTION 5

Be Inspired Every Day

"No one can make you feel inferior
without your consent."

-ELEANOR ROOSEVELT-

Introduction to Section 5

As we move on to developing your style next, an open mind is the most useful tool that you can take to this process. You will have worked out your body shape and may have been inspired by the section on colour to try something new and you will have an idea about which type of wardrobe best suits your lifestyle.

This process is a very safe place for you to explore lots of new ideas by adding to things that you already have and then seeing how they all sit together. You won't be reinventing the wheel. You will just be taking things that other people have tried and tested already, which takes the guesswork out of it for you.

However, it is very common to unconsciously dress the way you think that other people expect you to dress, so first, we are going to unpick that a bit with mindset work and look at the lies we tell ourselves which hold us back.

Then we are going to get into developing your wardrobe using Pinterest boards, and from there, we are going to create your signature style. You cannot get this wrong. You will start from the place you are at right now and move your thinking on a little bit at a time over the coming seasons, rather than making huge changes all in one go.

Trust the process, do the work and you will get the results.

CHAPTER 18

Challenging Your Mindset

Impress yourself

They say you have 7 seconds to make a first impression and while we all want to make the right impression on the people around us, the very first person you need to impress every day is the person looking at you in the mirror. What you see and how you feel just before you leave your bedroom every morning is what sets the tone for the day ahead.

Clothing is often viewed as trivial, and yes, of course, it can be. When it is bought in a mindless way that is driven by trends and in a manner that creates needless waste, it quite rightly gets a bad reputation. However, when clothing is used strategically, it can be the complete opposite. It

For it to become a habit that will require no thought or effort, you must show up every day ready to take on the world, even when nobody is looking.

empowers and gives you the confidence to approach the day with a positive and inspired mindset. It can help to set you up to achieve the results that you want from your day.

Your self-image

Whatever stage in life you are at, whether you are a young mother whose life has changed dramatically and is snowed under with the new responsibilities of raising a family, or whether you are going through the menopause and find that your body has changed shape, you will benefit from asking yourself a few questions before we get into developing your style. You might be surprised by the answers and by the things that you do subconsciously that are affecting the results in your life.

Your ideal life vs. now

Take a few minutes to visualise what your ideal life would look like. What would your job be? Where would you live? What hobbies would you spend time on? What would you do on your weekends? It is a very powerful exercise when you start living as if you are there already. Your life will start to change and you will move closer to that vision.

Then think about how you show up at the moment. Is it aligned to where you want to go? Do you plan what you are going to wear or do you get up every day and throw on the closest thing to hand? Do you take care of yourself, knowing that how you show up will affect your day?

For it to become a habit that will require no thought or effort, you must show up every day ready to take on the world, even when nobody is looking.

Can you think back to a regular day when you had a great day and got loads done? You felt like you were a badass at the end of it. Success leaves clues! How did you show up? I'm guessing you showed up ready to take it on and your day was planned and executed with military precision.

Then think about a day recently when you felt like you couldn't get out of your own way. You got up and stumbled through the day feeling disorganised and unproductive. We all have mornings when we wake up feeling that we didn't get enough sleep. If we throw on the nearest thing that comes to hand, promising ourselves that we will come back later to get ready for the day, there's only a 50/50 chance of it actually happening. However, if you hop out of bed and start with a daily self-care routine, have a shower and dress to inspire yourself, do your hair and makeup, you will walk out of your bedroom door feeling ready to take on the day, whatever it might throw at you.

Self-image questions

Have a read through the following questions and give yourself the time to really think about the answers you come up with. Some of them might surprise you. They will help you to become more conscious of the decisions you make about how you reveal yourself to the world and why. There are no right or wrong answers, this is just to help you get a deeper understanding of what makes you tick. These questions are food for ongoing thought. You may be able to answer some of them now. You may have to sleep on others. Keep them in mind as they help you to evolve. Over time, as your life changes, so too will the answers to these questions.

How important are other people's opinions of you?

Do you worry about what other people think of you? Do you allow them to impose their ideas on you of what you should wear, even if their taste is different to yours? Why do you think their opinion is more valid than yours? The next time you catch yourself thinking that somebody else's opinion is more valid than yours, just take a few minutes to think about why that is and make a promise to yourself to start believing that when it comes to you, it is your opinion that matters most.

How do you want the world to see you?

Do you want the world to see you as loving, kind, laid-back, inspiring, reliable, nurturing, thin, fit, sporty, business-like or a visionary? Or maybe something else? Have a think about this and decide what it is that you want to tell the world about you. What you want to say to the world should directly influence how you dress. If you are very clear about the story you want to tell in everything that you do, it will remove the confusion that might otherwise hold you back or slow you down. It will also help others to get the message.

What if the clothes you wore were just for you?

If you had a week to yourself and didn't have to worry about anybody else seeing you or wanting anything from you, what would you do with your time, what would you wear for yourself and how would you want to look and feel at the end of that week? This can tell you a lot about who you are deep down or remind you if you have forgotten. If there is a mismatch between what you want to get done and how you want to show up, there may be a bit of work to do to align the two.

How do you want to feel?

At different times, you want to feel a full range of emotions from relaxed, motivated, empowered, inspired, calm, romantic, energised, etc. You can encourage the full spectrum of emotions by paying attention to how you put things together and finish them off with individual touches like accessories or even the most appropriate scent for the occasion. When you have a busy life, make sure you plan your wardrobe in advance as it will make you feel relaxed and in control.

What makes you feel comfortable and uncomfortable?

What things do you put on and think, "this is me," and what things do you take off because they just don't feel right? When you do this work and really get in touch with who you are, you will understand why certain things, which look fabulous on somebody else, make you feel a bit ridiculous. That's perfectly normal. I've seen on so many occasions, two people of the same height, size and body shape put on exactly the same outfit, and while one will rock it, the other will look awkward. If you really love something but you find it's not quite right, ask a stylist to show you how to make it work for you.

What are you trying to get done every day?

I'm a firm believer in dressing for the day that you want to achieve. A very simple example of this is when you go to the gym, you wouldn't wear your suit, so you shouldn't wear your gym clothes to the office. Know what you want to get done each day in advance. To get the most out of your day, group together the tasks and projects that might require you to dress in a certain way. I often find that if I'm dressed to be inspired or to get business done, I cannot design in the same way. That context switching that you apply to your head needs to be applied to your wardrobe too.

Your family and friends

What do you want your family and friends to think of you? It is most likely that you enjoy dressing for your partner, and that is great as long as it feels good for yourself too. I draw the line there, however. Outside of that, you should dress for yourself and what you are trying to achieve. At no time ever should your children, family or friends dictate what you wear. They just need to know that you are happy, confident and constantly evolving. They need to support your choices, offering their opinions when you ask for them.

What job do you want?

What would be your perfect job? Dress like you have it already. There is nothing like a bit of reverse engineering. Decide what you want, believe you are there already and you will start to take the steps that are needed to get there. Dressing the right way is the low hanging fruit when it comes to empowering yourself. This creates an expectation of yourself and that is super powerful in spurring you into action. It also helps other people to understand your vision and you may be surprised by the number of people who will step up and help you to get there.

What do you want to achieve in your lifetime?

As with the above example of reverse engineering your ideal job, you can also do this with your whole life. When you look back at the very end of your life, what do you want your life to look like? Start living and showing up for it now. Show up like you already have your ideal life every day and you will find yourself taking the necessary steps to make it happen.

What would you like to attract into your life?

Whether it is your ideal job or the love of your life, you can start attracting it into your life now. Obviously, this doesn't mean that it will appear like magic, but if you start doing the work and being the person who will bring this goal into your life then you will succeed. For example, if you have a big vision, but you are hanging out in your tracksuit trying to hustle it into fruition, there is a misalignment. Or maybe you want to attract a new romantic partner, but you are not making an effort to work on yourself and show up as your best self every day, you could be missing so many opportunities for others to be attracted to the twinkle in your eye and spring in your step. Live the dream today.

How do you want to be seen in the workplace?

As workplaces become more and more casual and dress codes become more blurred, it is the perfect time to show up as yourself. When you do the work in this book, you will stand out from the majority of people who just won't. Life becomes a whole lot more interesting when people take notice. Remember the information in the earlier colour section and bear it in mind when you are showing up at work to make sure that you position yourself for the opportunities and outcomes that you want.

A little word on Naysayers

People are very opinionated. I shake my head in disbelief at this every day, especially on social media. Their opinions are none of your business, so ignore them! Send them love and let them move along!

Whatever your answers were to these questions, remember that as you evolve over the coming seasons, you can choose how you see yourself. You can decide who you want to be and then become that person.

You are a goddess if you say you are and you are not if you say you are not. The choice is yours and so is the reality. It doesn't matter if nobody else believes it as long as you do.

When you have moments of self-doubt, it is just your primitive brain showing up to protect you from change and to keep you safe from harm. Do not let it sit in the driving seat!

Remember, this process is a safe place for you to explore lots of new ideas, adding pieces to what you already have and then seeing how they all sit together. You won't be reinventing the wheel. You will just be trying things other people have already tried and tested, which takes the guesswork out of it for you.

CHAPTER 19

The 9 Lies We Tell Ourselves

I just need to quickly throw this little curveball at you here before you get into the most important part of creating your own personal style. You need to be aware of these little lies we tell ourselves. When they show up, nod and smile and thank them for trying to protect you. Then invite them to take a seat on the sidelines!

Lies and negative stories

These lies or unconscious biases can lurk beneath the surface where you may not even be aware of them. We see them all the time and our customers are often totally unaware of them until we bring them to their attention. Once you become aware of them and see how they are holding you back, you can choose to tell yourself a different story and open up all kinds of new possibilities.

Which ones do you recognise?

Lie #1 I'm too old...

Says who? You can be young until the day you die, and you don't need anybody else's approval or permission for this. If you think about it, no matter what age our body says we are, we can feel exactly the same on the inside in our 40s and 50s as we did in our 20s and 30s. You only start to feel old if you let society's expectations and biases influence you. There is nothing like laughter, learning and silliness to keep you young. I heard somebody say recently that her kids didn't think she was funny. Her answer was brilliant, she said, "Well, if I'm laughing then at least one person thinks I'm funny, so, clearly I am funny." Well, the same goes for being old, or being young. Now I'm not suggesting that you dress like a 20-year-old when you are in your 40s or 50s, but keep that young state of mind. Keep learning, keep evolving and seek out people who do the same.

Lie #2: I'm too short...

I would just like to reframe that for you. I've always thought that I'm too tall, so you really can't win. We have to be happy with what we've been dealt in life and work with what we've got. You can add height with you heels, I can't chop mine off! I can, of course, stoop to appear smaller and that's what I did for a long time, but I'm pretty sure you won't want to trade for that.

It might help you to think of height in a different way. When you see somebody tall wearing something that you love, stop and think, "What version of that would work for me?" It might sound a little bit cheeky, but take a photo and ask the staff or stylists in your favourite store how you could make it work for you.

Lie #3 I'll be happy and more confident when I'm thinner/more successful, etc.

Why wait? Why not be happy today?! This brings me right back to working with what you have. Today is all we can be sure of right in this moment.

I am not all sunlight and rainbows all the time, but there is something that I do which gets me into a great vibe every day and that is practising gratitude. Sometimes I forget to do it, especially if things are going well, but when I find myself slipping into any kind of negative thinking, I get back into the habit. I'm not going to get all preachy. All I want to say is that each morning, I start the day by listing ten things that I am grateful for – yes, that's right, ten. Three is too easy, ten makes you dig deep, especially on those days when you really are not feeling it.

I do it for everything. When you get focused on the things that you actually do like about yourself, you will automatically take small positive steps to point your ship in a different direction rather than feel negative about something and just make it worse, e.g. feeling unhappy about your weight and comfort eating. Practise being happy with what you have today and you will attract more of it tomorrow.

Lie #4: I need to have somewhere to go to justify buying that...

Why do you need somewhere to go? I first became aware of this with my mother (sorry for using you as an example, Mam :+)). She would keep an outfit together with a protective cover over it, only wearing it for special occasions. Even worse, she would not split the pieces up and wear them with other things. So, the outfit might get worn a couple of times a year. Why, oh, why???? If an outfit makes you feel great, why would you want to only wear it on special occasions? All that is required is a slight shift in thinking to change this scenario. If you only buy for special occasions, I can see why you might do this, but hopefully, at this stage, I will have talked you out of shopping like that. When you see things that you love and find yourself saying, “I just need somewhere to go to buy that,” ask yourself how you would style it for every day so that you could get lots of wear out of it. Wear the things that you love all the time and inspire yourself every day.

Lie #5 I'm not the kind of person who could do/wear that...

This thinking can really hold you back from evolving. We usually see it when a customer admires something that one of our stylists is wearing. The only difference is, the stylist does it every day. It has become second nature. When you find yourself having this thought, remember that whatever it is that has caught your eye can be worked into your existing wardrobe. Start with a subtle change that does not push you too far outside your comfort zone. As you become comfortable with that, push yourself a little further. Make it a habit so that you know you can move in any direction that takes your fancy!

Lie #6 I need my husband's/sister's/ daughter's approval...

Somebody else's approval should not be your number one concern when it comes to your individual style. When you are well connected to who you are and what you like, you can break away from the need to constantly seek approvalfrom other people. Why would you want to give your own power to decide who you are to others? That's not to say that you will never ask them what they think. But their opinions should be the icing, not the whole cake.

Wear the things that you love all the time and inspire yourself every day.

To give you an example, my daughter came down the stairs the other day to ask my opinion on an outfit that she was going to wear out that night. She was 98% of the way there with it, but something wasn't quite right and she didn't know what it was. All it took was a slight tweak from somebody who's opinion she respected for her to be 100% happy with it.

Also, remember that our kids sometimes like to see us in a certain way (old), but that's not necessarily how we see or want to see ourselves!

Lie #7 I can't afford/justify it...

This is usually something we hear from people who are not in the habit of valuing themselves enough, and it's not always in relation to expensive pieces. However, as you have got this far in the book, I am hoping that this is not you. When you stop impulse buying and start to be more strategic about both your wardrobe and the things that you want to wear every day to empower yourself, you will see that the things that you love are an investment in you.

Always stop and calculate the value per wear. For example, if you choose well when buying a coat or a jacket, you will be able to wear it with many different outfits for several years. This way, you can really justify buying something that you love and feel valued every time you wear it.

Lie#8: I'm not cool enough...

What is cool? Think about it. Is it really about what somebody is wearing or is it the way they are wearing it? Cool is an attitude. It is a vibe that you get from somebody who is confident and happy in their own skin. Everything they do rocks because they believe that they rock. They rock everything that they do, not just their style, and you can too!

If you think you are not cool and you want to be, make it your mission to evolve into someone who is. It might take a little time: you won't make changes overnight. Add a bit of attitude to your style and wear it with confidence. Know who you are and practise being confident in your opinions. Keep your eye on the goal and fake it till you make it. There is nothing like it for preventing you from becoming invisible as you grow older. Some of the coolest women I know are over 70!

Lie #9: I have too much black/I don't do colour

I just might have way too many words to write on this one! I have too much black. Says who? If you love black and you have a whole wardrobe of it that mixes and matches, way to go! When you are shopping for something new and it fits in with lots of other things that you have, why would that not be a good thing? When it comes to buying black for an occasion, it is a no-brainer as you can wear it for many different occasions and just accessorise it in different ways for each one. Job done!

It is a good idea on days when you are feeling tired to have pops of colour to soften the black, especially close to your face. This can be done with accessories, jewellery, scarves, etc.

When somebody suggests that you should wear colour, you mind may straight away think of vibrant colours. This is not necessarily true. It is very easy to inject a bit of subtle colour to even the most muted wardrobe. Here's our soft and earthy colour board again if you want to have a look to get some ideas:
https://www.pinterest.ie/marygrantdesigner/the-soft-earthy-colour-palette/

The "neutral" colour board is also a good place for you to hang out from spring through to early autumn.

CHAPTER 20

Developing Your Style

There is a system that I use to give visual briefs to my team when we are working on our seasonal campaign photoshoots. I put together a vision board of everything that I want the shoot to be, from the story I want to tell to the lifestyle I want to convey, and everything in between. Everything that inspires me gets thrown at the board, initially without any questioning as to whether it works or not. The curating comes later.

There are two things about doing this that struck me the first time I did it. Firstly, once they saw the boards of images, everybody got excited about the vision and immediately got what I wanted without further explanation. Secondly, and most relevant to this book, is that even though I knew what I wanted, every time I did this exercise, I got inspiration for my own wardrobe and became excited about moving it forward. It was almost like a form of wardrobe meditation. It allowed me the time to lose myself in the process and find new things that I loved. This helped me to inch my wardrobe forward season by season, adding a handful of new things to what I already had.

I am going to teach you that process step by step so that you too can get excited about developing and evolving your personal style, season by season, year by year.

Trust the process and work through the steps one by one. By the time we are finished, you will be empowered and inspired and will have a visual reference for your individual style for the next 6 months and beyond.

This is a process that you can use for individual occasions as well, whether it is planning a wedding, a party or anything else that you want to really get clear on your ideas for. Even if you are getting somebody else to do the work, you can gather the information and share it with them so that they can quickly understand your vision for the project.

Create the right environment to be inspired

For this chapter, you will need to set the scene in order to be inspired. When you do this well, the process will empower you, save you a lot of time in the long run and cut out wasteful unplanned purchases. Make the effort at this stage and I promise you will be rewarded later.

You will work best if you are the most confident version of yourself, as you are right now, while you work through the process. Dress in something that already makes you feel great. Do your hair and makeup. Wear your favourite jewellery and approach the whole process we are going to work through for the rest of this chapter as your most fabulous self.

Choose an inspiring music playlist and have your headphones at the ready. Some comfy chairs, candles and a "do not disturb" sign for the family will really add to the ambience and help you to get the most out of it. Basically, this section is where you will do all your exploring and getting inspired. An environment that enables that is a must. If you can't get it at home, go somewhere that you can. It's a great excuse for parking yourself in a coffee shop for a few hours or even for a girls' night away!

If you are working through this process with somebody else, I recommend that you do the work in this chapter on your own as I am going to send you down the rabbit hole to get inspired. This is a very personal part of the process. You don't want to be distracted by other people's opinions on what is right for you and you don't want the stress of having to constantly reject their ideas.

Build your vision board

If you don't already have a Pinterest account, go ahead and set one up. Then create a visual board called "My

Personal Style". If you are new to Pinterest, it is a really easy platform to use. You will find lots of short videos on YouTube that show you how to do this.

When your board is set up, you are going to start populating the board by 'pinning' all kinds of images that inspire you. Everything that you feel is relevant to you, including non-clothing images, will go on your board. We are doing this so that you have a board which inspires your whole life.

The object of the exercise is to come up with an aspirational lifestyle that may be a little stretch from where you are right now. We want to end up with a board that excites you.

What to pin to your board

- Start by going to the Pinterest board for your style type (chapter 9). Take anything from that which floats your boat and repin it to your own board.
- Then, remember the other style types that I suggested combining with your own style type? Go to those boards and repin anything that appeals to you.
- When this is done, you can then go to all the other boards that go with the book and repin anything that you want from those. You are not curating at this stage, so just go with it. Don't stop to think why you are pinning them, all you need to know is that they speak to you.

- Next, start adding everything that you use to complete a whole look, for example, hair, makeup, jewellery, accessories, scarves, etc. etc. When you are pinning hair and makeup, make sure that you have a think about what appeals to you for daytime, evening time and special occasions. Pin them all. This will save you having to think about such things every time you need them.

Check that you have covered all areas of your lifestyle from work to play to social occasions, hobbies and relaxation. You want to make sure that you have every eventuality covered.

Only when you have completed this pinning list should you look at your board. You should be getting excited at this stage. To explore even further, when you find an outfit that you love, click on it to see the suggestions that Pinterest has for similar images below. This is where you really go down the rabbit hole and find all kinds of goodies. You could spend hours on end doing this and you should spend as much time as you can doing it, even a few days, as these boards can inspire you for several seasons.

Now, take a break! Go for a walk. Anything that gives your brain a rest. Even sleep on it if you find that your head cannot take any more of it.

Curate your personal style board

Now that you have created your personal style board, it is time to curate it.

Looking at your board can you see a theme emerging? It should excite you and you should be seeing the same things appearing all over it. These are the things that underline your personal style. Your board should make you want to throw everything out and start from scratch. We are not going to do that, don't worry, but you should be really inspired.

What we want at the end of this process is a board that looks like your dream wardrobe but has a grounding in reality. By that I mean that your images of outfits are not too much of a stretch from where you are right now.

In the process of curating, we do not want to lose anything that you have saved already. If you pinned them, you did so for a reason, even if they are not going to be a part of your style personality in the immediate future. So, create a second backup board where you can move ideas to be revisited at a later date. What we want to do next is start moving things to your backup board that don't quite work for you or that you cannot imagine all working together in your wardrobe. Keep moving the things that don't really work with those that you are most passionate about.

When you are finished, just do a double check to make sure you still have all the necessary elements of your life covered. Only when you are sure you have finished this step should you move on.

Add some lifestyle to your board

You might well ask why I would be suggesting that you add lifestyle images to your board. You will see what it does for your board when you do it. It really helps you to have an aspirational vision of what you would like your life to look like.

When you know what the vision is, you are halfway there

So, go ahead now and have some fun adding things like interiors (especially closets!), food, flowers, jewellery, favourite perfumes, candles, houses, hobbies, places you want to visit, cars, men (if you are single, I've got a few hunks on mine, wink wink). You may find that your boards look aspirational rather than realistic. This is perfectly fine, they should be a bit of a stretch as that is inspiring. My board has the most amazing modern architectural homes, including one on a lake! It's good to have things that raise your expectations and allow you to dream a little.

To finish off the job, get a couple of current fashion magazines as well, just so you can see what the trends are. You are not going to be following these, you are just going to be aware. You don't need 20 different magazines. I recommend buying *Vogue* for this purpose. When you do this at the start of each season (we will go through that later), buy the February and September issues, as they are the ones with all the collections in them. You can take photos of anything that inspires you in the magazines, but please only post them to your vision board if they are of good quality. Nothing will dampen the sizzle of a fantastic board quicker than bad images. Just as an indicator of a well-populated board, you should have 200+ images when you are finished (my personal board has over 700) . The more the better, as long as they keep you focused on one direction and do not cause any confusion. If anything is confusing you, move it to your backup board.

Your personal style board is now complete.

You will be using it to create your wardrobe and be inspired on an ongoing basis, so keep adding to it as you see things that inspire you. You have done a huge chunk of work that will continue to inspire you for several seasons. You will, of course, need to do a summer and a winter version so that your wardrobe is always relevant. Each season, you will evolve your style a little as you pin new things. I recommend that you put Pinterest on your phone so that you can access your board any time, especially when you may have an unexpected opportunity to explore some stores.

CHAPTER 21

Creating Your Signature Style

Now you have added a visually inspiring board of all your favourite things to your mindset work, you are ready to start dressing for yourself first. This is the most inspiring thing you can do every morning.

I have had people say to me on several occasions that men are lucky, they can just wear a uniform. A shirt, trousers and jacket and they are done. They are always surprised when I say, "Women can have a uniform too." They are like *"what????"*

It's true. I have a uniform. Most people would be very surprised if they saw my wardrobe. I have a very curated selection of pieces that all work together, which I move on from season to season, evolving my style from one season to the next so that I don't get bored. When you have done this once or twice, it is the easiest thing in the world to do.

Use your vision board to create your signature style

From your Pinterest board, you will now have a clear idea of what your personal style looks like. Have to hand your lifestyle needs, which you calculated previously in chapter 18. This exercise will remind you of what you need in your wardrobe to cover you for every day. Remember, you want to balance work with home life and socialising.

Your personal style is the first consideration. This is what will make you feel your most confident, content, inspired and empowered self.

Your daily activity dictates the pieces that you will need.

Remember that if you are not already doing it, from here on, you will be dressing in a way that is true to you. You can do this slowly at first by adding little touches of the style that you most relate to. Over time, as you gain more confidence in your choices, you can make bolder statements and choices.

From your Pinterest board, there are a few questions we want to answer.

I have had people say to me on several occasions that men are lucky, they can just wear a uniform. A shirt, trousers and jacket and they are done. They are always surprised when I say, "Women can have a uniform too.

What is your personal style?

Try to sum it up in one sentence. This will help you to stay really clear. Maybe you would like to do the style quiz again here to see if it has changed after all the inspiration you have been getting while creating your Pinterest board. Here's the link again if you would like to see: *https://marygrant.com/style-archetype-quiz/*

So, you might say, "I'm a Sophisticate, but I add a little bit of Romantic for date nights and a bit of Provider when I want to get stuff done." Or you might say, "I'm a Rock Chick but I like to mix it with a bit of Bohemian when I want to feel more feminine and I have a bit of Sophisticate on standby for business meetings." You get the idea.

Which pieces do you have already?

These will form the starting point, the base on which you will build your wardrobe. They will also be your safety blanket while you start to evolve. You may well find, over the next few seasons, that you will want to pass them on as you evolve, but for now, you will hopefully have a good few things you are happy to work with. These are the items that will be on your building blocks list.

Which pieces are easy add-ons to your current wardrobe?

You will use these to start evolving your style. You are only going to move forward bit by bit each season. There will be no drastic changes and no dumping of whole wardrobes. The things on this list will keep you focused when you go shopping though. No more quick fixes and one-night stands in your wardrobe! These are the items that form your essential list.

Which pieces make your heart beat faster?

They are probably the things that you have admired before, but you admired and then walked on by. These pieces are going on your wish list and bit by bit over the seasons, as you cut out the mindless purchases, you are going to start saying yes to them! These are the pieces that will remind you that you are worth investing in.

Now you're ready for your wardrobe

When you have your wish list of what you need or want and you are feeling inspired by your board, you are now ready to tackle that wardrobe!

Section 5 Summary

You have covered a lot in this section. You now know and will have started to banish the lies that get in your way and prevent your fabulousness from shining brightly.

You have done some work on your mindset to help you make braver choices, which I hope you will have utilised when creating your vision boards. If you need to, take a few minutes to go back and add some braver choices, which you might have said no to initially. You can work towards them if needs be.

You will have created your vision boards and edited them down to the look that you are after for the next six months. Don't hedge your bets, get really focused on what you love right now. This is not a forever decision; you will be doing the exercise again in six months when the seasons change again. So, you will have ample opportunity to rejig or just evolve slightly then. The choice, as always, is yours.

SECTION 6

The Secret to Being Eternally Fabulous

"You can be gorgeous at 30,
charming at 40
and irresistible for the rest of your life."

-COCO CHANEL-

Introduction to Section 6

You will probably have realised at this stage that the secret to being eternally fabulous is evolving and never getting stuck in a rut. Like everything else, when you do a little bit of work at a time, you avoid the massive remodelling that will otherwise become necessary at some stage and all the stress that goes with it.

The very first time you work through this process, it will take a little bit of time for sure, but once you have done that work you will only need to revisit it twice a year, in February and September, right at the turn of the seasons.

Invest a little bit of time in yourself and do the work. The level of success that you achieve depends entirely on the work you put in. I promise, do the job well you will benefit from it every day, as you will spend less time thinking about what you are going to wear. The clarity that comes with good planning will eliminate buying mistakes and you will save the time invested many times over. You will also cut down on buying things that you don't need, which will save you lots of money.

Don't underestimate the effect of knowing who you are and what your personal style is. Investing in the things that inspire and make you feel valued and wearing them every day are huge benefits to your mindset and self-esteem.

There are three simple steps to constantly evolving and being eternally fabulous.

1. Assess

In the **Assess** chapter, we will be taking a good look at where you are with your wardrobe right now. You will be decluttering it, identifying which of your existing pieces will form the building blocks for your personal signature wardrobe, using everything that you have learned about yourself so far.

2. Evolve

In the **Evolve** chapter, we are going to choose things from your vision board to move your look forward and inject a little newness to your wardrobe. We are also going to have a look at hair and make-up to make sure that everything feels up to date and relevant.

3. Refresh

In the **Refresh** chapter, we are going to make sure that you are focused on what you need to buy. You will be doing this every six months, so you are not going to make drastic changes. It's the small changes that you can sustain every day that will have the most impact.

There are a few reasons we do our Assess | Evolve | Refresh at the very start of the season. Firstly, when we go shopping, we are the early birds and get the first picks of the new stock, which is always a thrill. If you wait, you could miss out on your size and what a disappointment that would be after all your hard work. Plus, the item that you missed will be the item that you will think about all season and kick yourself because you didn't act early enough. Again, I cannot tell you what effect the opposite has on your headspace. When you are first in there and nab that piece that you know is limited, you will walk taller every time you wear it. Also, over time, when you collect these pieces, you will have a wardrobe that is always unique to you. And the biggest bonus of having and loving things that are years old… nobody else will have them!

Secondly, we benefit greatly from the injection of newness at the start of a new season; it is a mindset thing. You will be the early adopter as such and that influences lots of other areas of your life, inspiring you to embrace change and stay current and up to date with new developments in a fast-changing world. If you haven't tried this yet, you may be a little bit sceptical but hopefully, at this stage, you will trust me on this.

Thirdly, you will get the longest time wearing your new pieces, especially if they are seasonal. If you love the winter, you can bring it in early by getting into your knitwear as soon as the evenings get chilly. If you love the summer, why wouldn't you start it early by getting rid of your winter boots and getting into lighter options. You can still layer up until the weather gets warmer. It's all about the mindset. I have often heard people complaining about the bad summer we had, when I thought it was great and the sun shone every day. You won't notice how much the sun shines if you are still wearing your winter clothes.

For the next three chapters, you are going to be using the three lists you wrote previously: building blocks, essentials, and wishlist.

CHAPTER 22

Assess

Assessing your wardrobe now so you can see exactly what you have that will form the foundations of your new personal style.

Assess and declutter your wardrobe

Ideally, you will have taken a little bit of time to absorb your boards and be already excited about getting stuck into your wardrobe. You probably already know what is staying and what is definitely going. If so, this is a great place to be in and you will already be feeling empowered. If not, spend a bit more time on your boards over a few days and fill them out with more lifestyle images that get you excited.

Why it's Important to Assess

Assessing and decluttering your wardrobe is the first crucial step in the process of evolving. It gives you the opportunity to stop and think about where you are at and where you are going. The Assess step allows you to declutter your wardrobe and your head, so that your way forward is clearer and more focused. Doing the job well will make you feel empowered and more confident. This affects every other area of your life, so please schedule the time to do it properly. You owe it to yourself.

When we Assess

I always do the Assess process at the beginning of February and the beginning of September each year. For me, it is the best time as this is when the new season collections start to appear in the stores. It is also the end of a season and this is when we are naturally getting a little bit bored with our wardrobe and looking for a bit of newness. Doing it early always makes me feel like I am ahead of the game. On the occasions when things get away from me and I do it later, I always feel like I am on the back foot. Feeling like you are ahead of yourself is always going to make you feel a lot more kickass. Having said that, whatever time of year it is when you pick up this book, get started straight away and you can get into the rhythm of the seasons later. There is just one exception that I would like you to be aware of. You should also keep an eye on your favourite brands in July and mid-December, as that is when they do early deliveries for the upcoming season.

Before we Assess

A bit of preparation and housekeeping before you start assessing your wardrobe so that you get the most out of this process.

1. **Get some long plastic boxes with lids.** I use the ones I used to store the kid's toys in. They fit nicely into an attic space, are great for storing out-of-season clothes and keep everything in one place.
2. **Invest in a set of matching hangers.** It sounds a bit obsessive, but get out of the habit of taking hangers with purchases that result in you having a wardrobe of mismatched hangers that your clothes slip off. This kind of preparation affects your headspace before you ever put a stitch into your wardrobe. I always recommend having matching hangers. They will make everything feel more special. Have a collection of clippy hangers for skirts and pants, and proper coat hangers for coats and jackets that protect the shape of the shoulders.
3. **Keep your wardrobe clean.** Once empty, properly clean down your wardrobe. Prepare it for the

coming season while it is empty. Additions like scented sachets add a touch of something special to underwear drawers, while lavender and cedar balls repel moths.

4. **Keep your wardrobe colour as neutral as possible.** This will ensure that it is your clothes that stand out rather than coloured paint or loud carpet. When the space is empty it should look like a blank canvas to show off your collection of clothes and accessories.

What to Assess

Using your 'building blocks' list, you are going to Assess every item of clothing in your wardrobe. It either stays, goes into storage or goes out the door. Then you are going to Assess your shoes, accessories, bags, etc. in exactly the same way.

How to Assess

We want to be ruthless at this stage; there is no room for dithering over whether to keep something or not. If you are not sure about whether or not to keep or get rid of something but you are not 'feeling' it at the moment, put it into storage.

If you are already in the habit of storing things that are out of season, great. If not, now is the time to start.

What you want to do is give yourself a bit of breathing space by removing the things that you are not going to wear for the coming season. They need to be stored clean and protected so that you fall in love with them all over again when you take them out the following season.

Assess each item in your wardrobe. Keep the pieces that transition between seasons. Keep the investment pieces that you still love. These are your no-brainers.

Once you have picked off this low hanging fruit, you are going to Assess every other piece in your wardrobe. With each piece, ask yourself: do you still want to wear it and is it part of the look that you have planned for the next season. Keep what you know is going to work. Put aside anything that is not part of where you are 'going'.

Sort into five piles:

1. Keepers
2. Storage
3. Sell
4. Donate
5. Recycle (not dump!)

Sort out the piles as you go along and put anything that is going straight into labelled bags in order to prevent overwhelm and potential meltdown as this is the worst part of the job!

Keepers: There will be pieces that transition across seasons, things like your jeans, leather jackets, shirts, etc. As long as you are still feeling the love for them, these useful and versatile pieces will be going straight back into your closet.

Storage: Put into storage anything that is specific to the season just finished. Make sure that the items are clean, folded and stored in such a way that you will be excited to see them again, not dreading the state they might be in. Fold delicates in tissue paper and make sure they are stored in airtight containers. Your woollens should have lavender or cedar balls, which are both a deterrent to moths. Try to keep everything stored in one place so that you do not forget what you have and end up buying things you don't need.

Sell: The things you do not feel the love for anymore may still have value, especially if they were investments at some stage. Somebody else may still get a lot of wear out of them and it's a great opportunity for you to get a few bob to put towards your next investments. One of the boutique buyers I know would sell every single piece in her wardrobe at the end of each season and buy everything new for the following season. She always had a nice little wad of cash going into the new season, and always looked great.

Donate: No doubt there will be things that you haven't worn in a while that won't be worth much but somebody will still get some use out of them. Donate these to friends or a charity shop. You could also have a swishing party. This is when you arrange an evening with your friends. You all bring pieces that you no longer have a use for and swop them among yourselves.

Recycle: The best fibres for recycling are 100% natural or 100% synthetic, as the technology for recycling mixed fibres has not yet been commercialised. Polyester can be recycled into new fabrics in the same way as plastic bottles, and things like denim can be mechanically recycled and spun into new fabrics. So, don't let anything go to landfill.

We still have a way to go before we will be able to recycle everything into new clothes, but initiatives are being run by some of the big players in the fashion industry to encourage innovation. So, if there is anything that you feel is beyond wearing, pop it in your nearest clothing recycle facility. You can find these in some supermarkets and wherever you see bottle banks.

Assess what you have in storage

Assess everything that you have in storage from the previous year (don't worry if you haven't been doing this so far, just skip this step for now). Everything that you still love, pop it into your wardrobe. Anything that doesn't fit with your look for the coming season but you are not ready to get rid of goes back into storage. The pieces you have already set aside which belong to the season that is just ending also go into storage.

You are already a winner when you get to this stage. If you did nothing else except replace the items that need replacing you are on the way to being the most inspired version of yourself.

Complete the Assess step

Your wardrobe may look a little bit sparse at this point. This is good! You should be starting to see where the gaps are that need to be filled. Don't rush straight into the next step without taking a bit of time to enjoy the bit of headspace that comes with this.

A great way to finish off this step is to 'merchandise' what you have. This means arranging things nicely in the space. Make sure that your hangers are all facing the same way and nicely spaced out if you have the room. Make sure that your shoes and accessories are arranged in such a way that they inspire you even when you are not wearing them. It will make everything that you have feel more special and you will really notice what is missing. If you added closets that inspire you onto your vision board, go back and have a look at them now to be inspired how to do this. Don't forget that these have been styled for photos so they are aspirational, but you will be able to adopt elements of them for your own wardrobe. To give you an example, I always hang garments that are alike together, such as coats, jackets, dresses, skirts, etc. My matching hangers are spaced 2 fingers apart and then, as a double check when I am finished, I take out anything that doesn't look like it can be worn in several different ways with several other items. I am ruthless about this, if it is in my wardrobe, it has earned its place.

"

I have been a Mary Grant customer for years and was recently headhunted as one of the team stylists. This process completely changed how I think of my own wardrobe. While I am good at putting things away out of season, I had stuff everywhere, on top of wardrobes, under beds. I was always forgetting about the things that I had. They are all going in the attic from now on.

-ANDREA HAMILTON-
Relationship Coach "

CHAPTER 23

Evolve

Finding new sources of inspiration so that you can effortlessly move forward season after season, year after year, without ever having a major overhaul on your hands.

Why it is important to Evolve

I have mentioned the reasons why we Evolve before, but it is worth reminding you again as you are now going into the Evolve stage. Evolving each season ensures that you always feel relevant as you go through the different stages in life. When you don't Evolve, it is like not maintaining your house. You will get away with it for a few years. However, slowly but surely over time, you will notice that things start to look tatty and unloved. Before long, you will feel that things are starting to fall apart, all at the same time. This is exactly what happens to your style and confidence over time when you do not pay attention to it. At that point, you know you are stuck in a rut. It can take months to get out of a rut and your confidence will take a huge hit while you are trying to get back on track.

When you evolve, you feel like you are on top of your game. You will not only feel relevant, but the little self-care routines that you put into place will make you feel valued, even on those occasions when you feel unappreciated. Looking after yourself builds your self-esteem, making sure that you feel fabulous, confident and ready to take on the world every day.

When We Evolve

Again, just a little reminder of why we do this at the start of each season. Everybody likes a bit of newness from time to time. When we are strategic and go through this process, we automatically update and inject that bit of newness as the seasons change, which is a time when we are naturally ready for change. When we start a new season with an updated version of ourselves, it is very powerful. That energy spreads to all other areas of our lives. That energy will keep us going until the next turn of the seasons, when we will be ready for change again. Working with this cycle will save us so much time as we have a system in place which will prevent a wardrobe sugar craving!

How I Evolve

Here's an example of what I do, to give you an idea of how to approach it. I mentioned before that my wardrobe has the following items in it from one season to the next: pinnies, dungarees, skinny jeans, Dr Martens, leggings, layering vests, shirts, knitwear. Each season, I will literally inch it forward by eyeballing a new pair of boots that will go with most of what I have already. I may decide that one of my new key items is a certain type of jacket that will change up my look a little bit. I will always update my basic layering pieces and I will work in a few new pieces to change up how I wear my layering wardrobe. I will update my shirts and update the tops that I wear under my pinnies. After that, I may have some favourites from our new collection that I am eyeballing and will be on the lookout for key individual pieces from other collections that excite me.

I also look at pieces that can transition across seasons. For example, my pinnies and dungarees never go into storage. I will wear them with white converse and white T-shirts in the summer and boots and knitwear in the winter. The same goes for things like jeans and jackets. I am always on the lookout for these pieces which I invest in guilt-free and reinvent each season. It only takes a handful of new pieces to satisfy the want for newness, when they are the items that you really want.

Depending on the season, I may do some or all of these things, but once I am moving it forward that is what I am trying to achieve.

I always make sure that I am covered with two or three outfits that I can dress up for an event. In the past, these occasions used to stress me out as I always invest in what I wear every day. Over the last few years, however, I realised that by having a few simple pieces I can dress up with statement earrings or necklaces and wearing my hair in a slightly more dramatic way, I am covered for most occasions.

Use your wishlist to Evolve

Now that you have your 'building blocks' from the last chapter, you will be using your 'wishlist' from chapter 22 for the Evolve stage. This is the list that you will use to move your style forward a little bit. I hope you are excited! It is also a good idea to have your vision board handy to remind you and reassure you as you work through this stage.

The main things to think about as you are deciding which pieces from your list and board you are going to prioritise are:

Take a special note of the things that set your soul on fire. These should be at the top of your wishlist. The cheap version of anything will never be as satisfying as an original – don't say I didn't warn you. There is something about investing in an original piece that makes you feel amazing and it is worth the investment every time you wear it.

What are the things that keep cropping up on your vision board that you are not wearing yet? These are no-brainers and you will start to see them everywhere. If they have cropped up in lots of different outfits and you see people wearing them in different ways, then you know they are going to be versatile enough to be a good return on your investment. For example, after creating the vision boards to go with the book, I already have lust list for next season.

Note the accessories on your board that you can use to change the emphasis of an outfit; for example, layering jewellery pieces will create a very different look to one big statement piece.

The things on your board that are a bit of stretch for you right now stay on your board. Let them continue to inspire you and they may make it to your shopping list at some stage in the coming seasons.

Things to remember when Evolving

You are aiming to move your wardrobe on not change the whole thing. If you have a long list of things that you want to buy, great! That means you are really inspired and have done the work. Just prioritise the pieces you will get the most wear out of.

As well as the physical, make sure that you are covered for the way you want to feel as well. For example, if you want to rev things up in your working life, make sure you have prioritised some pieces that will make you feel like you are upping your game. If you need to relax more, make sure you have prioritised some beautiful loungewear. If you want to attract a new partner, invest in some things that make you feel feminine every day.

Make sure that you have your lifestyle well covered. You don't want to find that you have 20 outfits for work and nothing to inspire a relaxing weekend or 20 outfits for going out and nothing to inspire a successful weekday. Note where your gaps are in your lifestyle wardrobe and make sure that they are top of your shopping list.

You want to be aiming to have at least five key pieces in your wardrobe that can change up different outfits, which you will be excited to wear and remind you that you are worthy of investment.

The pieces that will be most versatile are coats, jackets, statement dresses (especially if you can layer them), handbags, accessories, shoes/boots and any signature everyday pieces that make you feel like your most confident and inspired self when you wear them. These are your investment pieces. Buy them because you love them and you will be able to rework them season after season and year after year.

Consider your personal style in footwear. Again, you don't want to be buying twenty pairs of shoes. It is a great plan to have 2 great pairs of classic shoes in your wardrobe for social and special occasions, a black pair and a nude pair. There are very few outfits that you can't wear one or the other with. If shoes are your thing and budget is not an issue, you can of course have a whole wardrobe of shoes, but otherwise, you don't need specific shoes to go with every colour and outfit in your wardrobe. Save your budget for great shoes that you can wear every day.

Each season when you are Evolving, note any special occasions and life events that are coming up in the next six months, family weddings, big birthdays, etc. Prepare in advance for them. Don't wait till the last minute and put yourself under pressure. As with anything, preparation will take the stress out of these events and as with everything else, when you are prepared in advance, you will always spend less, saving more of your budget for everyday fabulousness.

What else do you need to Evolve?

Evolve your hair

Move your hair on in the same way that you move your wardrobe on so that you don't get stuck in a time warp. There will always be a variation on what you are doing that will inch you forward. Again, we are not talking about drastic change here. As you get older, pay attention to your skin tone and when you find that the greys are reappearing so fast that your 6-week touch-up is not doing the job any more, there has never been a better time to rock grey. If you are thinking of making a big change to your hair, search for some ideas and pop them on your vision board. Watch out for images of people with a similar shape face and similar hair texture. Live with it on your board for a while and see how it fits into everything else that you love before you take the leap. Now is also a great time to make sure that you have a couple of evening hair-style options on your board, so that you don't have to think about it when you have an event.

Evolve your make-up

Be sure to pin some makeup images to your vision board. Each season, do something new to revive your look, even if it is only a different eye palette or a new lip colour. Every season arrange a makeup appointment with your favourite makeup counter to see what is new. Pick a forward-thinking brand that caters to all age groups and will be able to give you tips on the most relevant palettes. You can book a full makeover for the price of a couple of products, so you will get a lesson and new product for the price of a lunch out with a friend!

Keep Evolving

Each season, revisit your storyboards and do another little search to update it with what is speaking to you at the time. Install Pinterest on your phone and keep adding to your board when you see something that you like so that you are not starting from scratch every season. This really does help you to consistently and organically evolve your wardrobe.

Each stage of your life – from being a student to building a career, raising a family, to empty nests and maybe caring for elderly parents – will require a different version of you to be in the driving seat. You must Evolve or you will keep getting stuck, wrecking your own head and wasting valuable time. Keep moving and don't look back.

"

I used to have a very romantic style, I wore lots of floaty layers. When I found myself running around after three kids, my wardrobe became a lot more practical. When they got to an age when they needed me less, I decided to dip my toe back into the working world and have recently set up my own interior design company. I needed to find a signature style to go with it. Mary's collection provided a capsule of mix and match jerseys that make me look and feel great, while being practical for the long physical days going from client to client and overseeing projects. I also love her unstructured shirts which I can mix in with my jeans for an edgy and creative look.

-ADELINE MOLLOY-
Interior Designer "

CHAPTER 24

Refresh

Prioritising your needs and creating your shopping list

Why is it important to Refresh?

Now that you have Assessed what you have and decided what the key items are that you will use to Evolve your style, it is time to decide what you are going to spend your budget on and write your shopping list.

Even on those occasions when you are on a tight budget, you can Refresh your wardrobe with basic items like underwear, T-shirts, hair and makeup. These are all small ticket items that are very satisfying. My kids always joke that there is nothing like putting on new underwear or socks for them to feel like the day is off to a great start. (I promise I don't brainwash them!)

By the time you have created your wishlist, you may already know what you want to invest in for the coming season and if so, that is great! Maybe top of your list is a pair of boots or a leather jacket that will reinvent 10 items that you already have? Maybe it is a few new T-shirts to go with your favourite jeans. Whatever your focus is, start writing your shopping list, prioritising the pieces that you are definitely going to buy.

Some things to be mindful of in the process of Refreshing your wardrobe

Investment pieces are investments in your confidence

When you buy the best that you can afford and buy investment pieces, you will feel amazing every time you wear them because you have invested in yourself. You will be able to mix them with less expensive pieces and still feel the effects. Buy them early and enjoy them all season long.

You can adapt your investment pieces each season, moving them on over time. You can change them up by adding accessories, pops of colour and introducing new pieces that change your look slightly, completely rejuvenating your whole wardrobe and keeping it interesting. Over the lifetime of investment pieces, they really will serve you well and make you remember that you are worth it.

Comfort dictates energy

I will go into all the different types of fabrics in the last section, but here I just want to say that there is a reason why our stretch fabric pieces are always our bestsellers. Perhaps, without realising why, people gravitate towards them. Everything from jackets to jeans, skirts and dresses, you won't get anything as comfortable as fabrics that have even a small percentage of stretch in them. Whatever the situation or what you are getting up to, they help you to look great without feeling restricted.

I am a firm believer that what you wear next to your skin should feel like a second skin. Choose soft fabrics that return to their original shape when you give them a good stretch. If you are conscious of your clothes during the day, you are being distracted from the more important things you need to be thinking about.

Colour

If you don't wear a lot of colour normally, don't forget to add in a few strategic pieces from our colour psychology section. What a great boost to your day to whip out something yellow or orange when you need a creative boost or to inspire those around you. Scarves are a great way to do this.

Hot & cold

We all feel heat and cold in different ways. Whether you are a cold creature or hot stuff, there will be times in your life when your body temperature misbehaves, causing you stress and getting you hot and bothered. The best way to control this is to wear light layers that you can put on and take off as the need arises.

Natural fibres like silk, linen and cotton are best for keeping you cool. Modal, while not a natural fibre, is also good for regulating temperature while absorbing moisture.

Wool is the obvious choice for heat along with light-weight down outerwear. But for a bit of lightweight heat which can be layered Summer or Winter, treat yourself to a cashmere wrap. They are multipurpose, serving as a wrap to complete an outfit, a scarf in the depths of winter, a travel companion to snuggle up with for a snooze on flights, a layer to keep handy for air-conditioned buildings or even to snuggle up with for an evening on the couch. They are a touch of luxury that will make you will feel amazing every time you wear them.

Look after your feet and they will look after you

Not everybody will agree with my philosophy on footwear. To put it quite simply, it should be comfortable. I am not a believer in wearing crippling shoes for the sake of glamour. On occasions, they are fine, but always have a second pair that you can change into. Whatever stage you are at in life, your feet will thank you if you look after them. Heels can cause backache and make you more tired at the end of the day than you might be otherwise. Completely flat shoes can cause painful fallen arches over the course of time. Wearing boots all the time can also cause problems as they restrict the natural heel to toe movement when walking. If you are on your feet all day, make sure your shoes have good support and absorb shock well.

Refresh your wardrobe: checklist

Refresh your layering pieces

A great way to transition between seasons is to layer up. You never know what the weather might throw at you, so, it's good to be able to add or take away a layer as necessary. They are also great for adding interest to an outfit.

Refresh your travelling pieces

Lightweight mix and match pieces that can be worn a few different ways can take a lot of the stress out of travelling, and cut down on the amount of luggage you will need to bring. Keep an eye out for holiday pieces when you are not under pressure to find them. Ideally, you should never have to go shopping for any of these. With clever 'spotting' you will always be ready to go. Pick pieces that work in with your everyday wardrobe so that you are getting lots of wear out of all your purchases.

Refresh your underwear

Great outfits start with good underwear. Wear the right inner layers for your outer layers. There are so many different types and there is no excuse for knicker lines. There are few people who wouldn't benefit from having some control underwear in their wardrobe. Control pants and contour leggings are designed to hold everything in place and create a smooth base for everything that goes on top. They will not only make you feel super confident, but ensure that everything looks better. It is well worth allocating some of your budget for these confidence boosters. The other thing I will say about underwear, buy it for yourself and have a few cheeky sets for those days when you want an extra injection of confidence.

Refresh with a coat

As with everything else, buy coats because you love them, and get them early in the season so you are not taken by surprise with that first cold snap. Choose the more unusual ones that work with your default colour scheme for timeless basic looks. Even if the Winter is mild that particular year, you will have your coats for decades and always have something to match whatever you are wearing. Coats are also the exception to sticking to a similar palette of colours. A bright colour will improve your mood on the dreariest winter's day and add a touch of wow and wardrobe envy to your look, especially if you wear a lot of black.

Refresh with a statement jacket

A good jacket is something that you will have for many years. If it is a work jacket, something a little bit more than the basic tailored jacket will make you stand out from the crowd, both physically and mentally. They are worth investing in as you will get great value per wear over time. They can also be really cool worn as part of a more casual off-duty outfit.

Refresh with handbags

You will get away with mixing cheaper with more expensive pieces and nobody will ever know or believe it if you are wearing a fab handbag. They are worth investing in and will even inspire you when they are sitting on a shelf in your wardrobe.

Refresh with jewellery

There is nothing like a new piece of jewellery to make you feel really special. There are lots of options that won't break the bank that will not only make you feel great, but will also finish off lots of different outfits. And I'm not suggesting that you should wait for somebody else to buy it for you, buy it for yourself!

Refresh with accessories

Hats and scarves are great for bad hair days.

Statement jewellery pieces can be used to dress up simple outfits for events or to change up the look of a simple neckline. Little add-ons can create whole new outfits and are a great pick me up on a day when you just need a little treat. Sunglasses are not just for summer but are great for injecting a bit of attitude all year round.

Refresh your tights and socks

A selection of tights can change up lots of different outfits. A simple dress worn with opaques during the day can be transformed with a pair of sheer tights for evenings. Patterned tights can add an element of fun to an outfit and a contrasting colour can be a statement with an otherwise very plain outfit. Pay attention to your socks too. They can be used to add a touch of quirkiness to your wardrobe.

Refresh your hair and makeup

I've already mentioned these in the last chapter. This is just a little reminder. I always like to do this before I go shopping for anything on my list as it is always a confidence booster and puts you in a great place to be inspired when you are shopping. It can also be a great way to hold yourself accountable to a deadline to get the job done. So, it's worth popping a date in the diary ahead of time for the start of each season.

Refresh your basics

Basics will mean different things to different people, depending on what your style type is, but include everything that is essential to complete your outfits. Examples are your T-shirts, layering pieces, leggings, etc. Whites need to be upgraded regularly as, even with the best care, they will discolour over time. The sales are a good time to top-up on basics or keep an eye out for basics bundles, which is where you can get several basics pieces together at a discounted price. I cannot tell you how many brands might do them, but we will be doing them from AW19 on our jerseys, subject to availability.

Refresh your nails

If you like to wear nail polish, then update your colours each season and keep them season relevant. Darker, nude and neutral colours work well all year round, as do reds. Plums and aubergines and autumnal colours are lovely in winter, while pinks and pastels are perfect for spring and summer.

Refresh your skincare

I do not claim to be an expert on skincare, not by any stretch of the imagination, but we have different requirements in summer to winter, so update your needs as the seasons change.

Refresh your perfume

Maybe you are like me and have one perfume that you use all year round. I even have a bottle of it on my desk for a little pick me up during the day. It's a little effortless reminder that I'm worth it. If you like to try new things, the start of each season is a good time to make a change. Have a little squirt of a different scent as you are passing through department stores coming up to a new season to see what's new and what suits the upcoming season. There are different notes to suit summer and winter.

Create your shopping list

Make your shopping list and keep it with you. Put the Pinterest app on your phone so that you can refer to your vision board at any time and pop your shopping list into the notes on your phone. Together they will stop you getting sidetracked by trends and quick fixes. You will want to have it to hand for those unexpected opportunities to browse.

Be ready for pieces that you find when you are not looking for anything in particular. These are always the best finds. They are the pieces that you will love for years. The best time for browsing and finding those gems is when you are already inspired by what you are wearing. So, if you are meeting a friend for lunch, give yourself an extra hour for popping into a few shops on the way. Lots of our customers pop in on their way from getting their hair or nails done, or even on the way from the gym. These are all times that people seem to be inspired. Everything that makes you feel good is an inspiration.

Section 6 Summary

Well done, you have done the most physical bit and you probably need a little lie-down or a big glass of wine or other favourite bevvy.

You have Assessed what you already have that will form the building blocks of your wardrobe going forward.

You have Evolved by deciding how you are going to dress for the next six months or until the season changes at least. You have noted any occasions that are coming up. Having that work done will leave you prepared for any other surprises that come out of the blue, which is going to save you a lot of time and stress, happy days!

You should now be excited to go shopping with your curated shopping list from the Refresh process. Don't worry if not, you can just go back to the beginning and start again… just kidding. If you do need more help, don't worry. There are ways that we can give you more help and make sure that you nail your personal style. I will tell you about that in our very last section.

Even if you are not 100% confident enough to rock your own personal style at this stage, this is only the start of the journey. You will have so much information under your belt that will help you to start making better choices and with practice, you will get a step closer every day.

SECTION 7

Top Tips

"Buy less. Choose well. Make it last."

-VIVIENNE WESTWOOD-

Introduction to Section 7

This is a reference section of useful hacks and insider tips. Some of these things you will know already. Some of them I have learned over my 25 years of serving customers.

Top styling tips are a list of things to remember. When you practise them often, you will be confident in your choices and worry less about what other people think.

Top shopping tips will keep you on track with creating your outfits and ensure that you don't miss out on the best pieces for you. Stick with them and you will save not only money but lots of the most precious commodity of all... time.

Top garment care tips will save you lots of time while ensuring that you get the longest life possible out of your clothes.

CHAPTER 25

Top Styling Tips

Creativity never goes out of style

You will find that when you are true to what you love, the things that you buy will usually work together, even when you imagine they might not.

I gained absolute confidence in this theory when we were setting up our flagship store. I knew I didn't want to copy anything that I had seen before, but I wasn't quite sure what look I wanted to achieve. I had been gathering furniture pieces that I loved, just because I loved them. I knew that they were for a shop, but did not know where that shop might be or what the end result would look like. This went on for about three or four years.

When the time came to find a location for the store, I didn't do what you would expect and create a mood or storyboard. Instead, I took everything that I loved and moved them into the space in the middle of the night so that if they didn't work, I could get them back out without anybody seeing them! There was a mixture of antique chairs, ornate mirrors, industrial electrical cable reels, galvanised steel rails, handmade velvet curtains, toile de Jouy wallpaper and an old wood worker's bench. It sounds like a car crash and having a plan would have been a lot less stressful. But I wanted something that was unique to our brand, without being influenced by any images of other stores. It was risky but it worked.

My point here is that when you have completed all of the previous work, you will have a very good understanding of what you like and why. When you get to that point, completing your outfits becomes much easier. You can gather things that you love with confidence and know that they will all work together, creating a look that is unique to you. That is true style and will never date.

Top styling tips:

1. Be your own style icon

When you have decided what style you are going for, make a list of the pieces that are essential to pin it down. You are not looking for an instant wardrobe, so take your time and invest in your iconic style pieces.

2. Attitude

Whatever your favourite style type, like everything else, preparation is everything. When you are in control of your wardrobe rather than feeling like it is controlling you, this positively affects every aspect of your life from morning to night. Putting the work into strategically planning how you are going to present yourself to the world will serve you well.

3. Embrace your shape

There are no hard and fast rules when it comes to your shape. Just remember to focus on your best bits and divert attention away from the parts of you that you might not be so comfortable with. Everybody has something that they like and something that they don't love so much about the package they are given. We are all imperfect humans, so get over it. Go back to the "know your body type" chapter and follow the guidelines for your shape. Mastering this is the key to having great confidence.

4. Layers

Remember, when it comes to layering, the key rule is to make sure that your base layer is a good close fit. Loose under layers will make you feel swamped. A close fit underneath will show your body shape while also allowing you the comfort that comes with layering. Invest in good jerseys, they will serve you well for this purpose. Cheap jersey pieces with poor elasticity are not going to last or feel as good as the best ones which will last for a long time when you care for them properly. Then layer lighter layers on top and in cooler weather, finish the look off with a cosy knit or jacket.

6. Undies

The base upon which you build any outfit is very important. There is a personal relationship between you and your underwear, so put a little bit of thought and planning into how you put it together. Wear matching sets. This says that you value yourself and makes you feel more confident and purposeful from the inside out. Wear underwear that inspires you and makes you feel a little bit cheeky. Nobody will know, only you, but it will make your day a bit more fun.

Make sure that you wear the correct sizes and replace any underwear that is past its best.

7. When in doubt, go nude

If you are unsure of what kind of underwear you should be wearing, going nude is a safe bet. Nude underwear also applies to pale coloured tops that might be a little bit see-through. The nude rule can also apply when you are matching shoes to an outfit, especially if it is for an occasion. These are worth investing in as they will last for years. I have a gold pair (which come under the nude category) from a photo-shoot in 1995. They still come out for shoots and special occasions and they go with loads of things.

8. *Loose & tight*

You may be somebody who loves to just cover everything up and have a personal relationship with your body. That is between you and your clothes and it is perfectly fine. If you are more body-conscious, you might like the idea of wearing looser-fitting clothes but feel a bit swamped by them. The trick here is to wear loose-fitting pieces with tighter-fitting pieces. For example, you could wear wide pants or a flowing skirt with a fitted top or vest. Or you could do the reverse and mix skinny bottoms with an oversized top. Whatever body shape you are, one of these versions will work for you.

9. *Show skin strategically*

As with everything, less is more. Showing skin in too many places is a big distraction. Don't be surprised if people's eyes dart all around the place. There is a rule in photography, you remove anything that distracts the viewer from the main subject. If you have too much going on, the viewer does not know where to look. It is distracting so they will go from one area of the photo to another, not

There is a personal relationship between you and your underwear, so put a little bit of thought and planning into how you put it together. Wear matching sets. This says that you value yourself and makes you feel more confident and purposeful from the inside out.

really understanding what it is the photographer wants them to look at. Apply the same principle to how you dress. Keep it simple, do not show it all at the same time and don't be surprised if when you show it, people look at it. If you don't want them to look at a specific area, draw attention to a different area!

10. Tailored jackets

Every wardrobe will benefit from having a couple of well-tailored jackets that work with your style. They transform a relaxed comfortable outfit that allows you to get things done into something that is instantly a bit smarter when the situation arises.

11. LBD

Whatever your style, every wardrobe needs a little black dress. When you have one, you will never be stuck for something to wear for those unexpected invitations or events that creep up on you. They can be changed up from one event to another just by changing the accessories that you wear with them.

12. From every day to occasions and back again

Remember when you have done the work up until now to make your wardrobe timeless, you are always just a couple of tweaks away from taking an existing outfit that you get lots of wear out of and making it into something that will take you to those unexpected occasions. The same goes for buying an outfit for an occasion. Invest in pieces that you will wear time and time again.

13. Check full length & rear

A full-length mirror is an essential part of any wardrobe. This is one of my personal non-negotiable rules. Use it every day. Check how everything works together from head-to-toe and don't forget to check the back view. If you can have a second full-length mirror, place it near the front door so you can check everything last thing before you leave the house, which will ensure that any self-doubt is left at home.

14. Hem trousers for specific shoe height

You don't have to have specific shoes for specific outfits. However, it is a good idea with trousers to hem them for the height shoes that you see yourself wearing with them. You might want to wear heels with tailored pants, or you might want to wear platform trainers with your wide-leg palazzos. If you want a certain style of pants to work with different heel heights from high to flat, invest in two pairs the same and hem them accordingly.

Whatever your style, every wardrobe needs a little black dress. When you have one, you will never be stuck for something to wear for those unexpected invitations or events that creep up on you.

15. When wearing white, check the light

White is a fabulous colour to wear. Don't be afraid of it. It makes a statement of not being afraid of standing out. There are just a couple of things to bear in mind to do it successfully. Firstly, you need to consider what to wear underneath. Invest in some long jersey shorts and pristine close-fitting jersey vests, which are a perfect base cover-up for anything that you might wear on top. You don't want them to interfere with the outfit, so do make sure that they are close-fitting, especially your vests. Check how see-through your outfit is in daylight so that you are not caught out when you go outdoors.

16. Wardrobe of shoes

Be strategic in choosing your shoes. Which styles go best with your chosen style type. Don't buy countless pairs of shoes that are all the same until you are covered with the different types you will need for different occasions and outfit types. Be kind to your feet, buy the best that you can afford. Make sure that they are a good fit and have both support and cushioning. Wearing the wrong shoes can leave you exhausted at the end of the day when you could otherwise have extra power in your batteries for all those other things that you THINK you don't have time for!

17. Accessorise with colour

A great way to introduce a pop of colour if you don't want to invest in brightly coloured clothes is to do it with a lipstick or piece of jewellery. A bright red lipstick can add a bit of glam to any outfit and there are lots of fabulous costume jewellery pieces which won't cost the earth. Costume jewellery is also a great way to draw attention to your eyes. Use the tips in the chapter on wearing colour.

18. Create your own look book

Take selfies or photos of outfits styled on hangers, whatever works for you. Print them off into a little notebook or save them on your phone or create a quick reference so you don't have to keep rethinking your outfits.

19. Change up your outfit with a scarf

Scarves are a great way to change up a simple outfit. As with everything else, keep an eye out for them when you are not under pressure to complete an outfit. Create a little wardrobe of them in different shapes and colours. They can also double up as hair bands and ties on handbags to complete outfits.

20. Be creative with jewellery

A great way to add individuality to your outfits is to mix it up with your accessories. Mix your timeless investment pieces with costume jewellery.

You can also layer your jewellery. Mix silver and gold and other metals. Start with just a couple of pieces and build your confidence. Layer different length necklaces to dress up various necklines. Longer pieces can also be worn wrapped twice for versatility.

CHAPTER 26

Top Shopping Tips

Shopping is one of those activities that most people either love or dread! I am hoping, at this stage, that you will be so excited about your personal style and so motivated by your shopping list that you will be a woman on a mission. I was getting excited curating the vision boards and writing the shopping lists and I am not somebody who likes to spend a lot of time shopping. So, if you want a fresh burst of inspiration at any time, go back to those.

Here are my top 20 shopping tips:

1. *Take advantage of personal styling in stores where it is offered*

Ask boutiques and department stores if they offer personal styling sessions. You will find that there are always opportunities at certain times of the day when the store is quiet for you to have the undivided attention of the staff. This is a great opportunity to pick stylists' brains on updating your wardrobe. They are only too happy to fill quiet times as everybody likes to be busy!

2. *Build relationships with in-store stylists*

Find somebody who has a similar style to yours or to what you want to achieve and let them get to know you. A good stylist will ask you lots of questions so that they can dig deep into your personal style. They will help you to match pieces that you have already with items from newer collections. When you have a relationship with a stylist, they will be able to give you a call and let you know when they have something new in that you might like to try.

3. *Wear something that inspires you*

When you dress in a way that inspires you, you will naturally find more of what you love. It's all in the state of mind. Have you ever found a piece that you loved when you weren't looking for anything in particular? It just completely worked with what you were wearing on the day? You can intentionally replicate that. For example, if you are looking for a leather jacket, wear an outfit that you imagine yourself wearing with it. If you are looking for a new pair of boots, wear what you imagine yourself wearing with them. You get the idea.

4. *Wear your good underwear*

Always wear good underwear when you go shopping. Everything looks better when you start with a good base. You wouldn't believe the number of people we have sent shopping for a good bra when they have come in to try on. You won't feel good about anything in bad underwear.

5. *Go handsfree*

Shopping can be very tiring especially if you are on a mission, traipsing around shops. Consider wearing a cross body bag rather than carrying a handbag which can result in backache. It also leaves both hands free for a good rummage and a better shopping experience. Most stores operate a collect service, so don't carry bags around with you if you can avoid it, just collect them all at the end of the day. You could alternatively ask the store if they can deliver. It

When you dress in a way that inspires you, you will naturally find more of what you love. It's all in the state of mind.

won't cost much and can be a lovely luxury shopping experience for you!

6. Open your mind

When you see something that you find interesting but are not quite sure how you would wear it, ask the sales staff or stylist on duty how they might style it. They are always more than happy to share their ideas and will have lots of tips from seeing other people trying on too.

7. Leave the guilt at home

You will know by now that I am a firm believer that when you feel amazing, everybody around you benefits from it, including any significant others in your life! So leave the guilt at home, feeling good is an investment in all your personal relationships!

8. Too many cooks!

Avoid going shopping with friends whose style is different to yours... They can all too often steer you away from the pieces that are perfect for you because they don't connect with them in the way that you do. If shopping for a special occasion, choose one or two people who really get your style and avoid asking other people's opinions. Nothing will melt your head quicker!

9. About fit

When you find a new brand, not knowing their sizing may prevent you from shopping with them initially. However, in this hyper-connected world, you will find that brands will be happy to discuss their fit with you online either through their websites or their social media. Take the chance and order something if you love it, be assured that if you do not have the opportunity to try something for fit, you will be able to return it for a full refund. (Always check the stores' policies as return windows vary from store to store.)

10. Go down a size in jeans

When in doubt about which size you should go for in jeans, choose the smaller pair. They always stretch after a few wears. This is especially true of stretch jeans. If you don't have to wiggle into them the first time, chances are they are going to be too big after a few wears!

11. Quality test your base layers and jerseys

Always stretch test your jerseys before you buy them. I'm not talking about knitwear here, but the jerseys that you wear close to your skin, especially leggings and close-fitting T-shirts. They should have a good 'return'. This means that when you stretch them, they should go straight back to their original size without any stretch marks. You should look for about 3-4% elastane on the care label. Stretchy fabrics without elastane have a mechanical stretch and won't hold their shape as well.

12. Consider wear and tear

Not only should you consider wear and tear on fabrics when you are buying them, also be careful when choosing garments with hardware or Velcro. These can spell disaster around your finer fabrics so make sure and keep them separate. I cannot tell you the number of times I have seen precious garments destroyed from wearing them with other garments which have Velcro, sequins, crystals, zippers, etc. This doesn't mean don't buy them, just exercise common sense and caution when you're wearing them.

13. Cashmere

You will know pure cashmere when you touch it, it is like nothing else you will ever touch. Not all cashmere that is labelled pure cashmere actually is! If it feels like wool, it is not pure cashmere. If it is cheap, it is not pure cashmere. If it is cheap, it has not been sustainably sourced either.

14. Accessories

When you just don't have a budget for shopping and you need a little treat, those are the days to check out accessories shops. A funky pair of tights, a coloured scarf that will go with lots of different things, a pair of earrings or even a bottle of nail varnish can all transform existing outfits. Bring your look book with you and check out your Pinterest board as a reminder of what you have that could benefit from a little update.

15. Check inside

You can tell a lot about the quality of a garment by looking inside. Quality will look good on the inside too with well-finished seams. Linings should be good quality. Another good indicator is the buttons. Quality pieces will have good quality buttons which are often hand sewn on.

16. Check the care labels

Always check the care labels before you buy. Be aware of how the garment should be cared for before you buy it. Always follow the instructions on the label, which will have been researched and tested by the brand.

17. Zippers

Zippers can tell you a lot about the quality of a garment. Cheap zippers will have rough teeth. When a zipper has smooth teeth and glides open and closed without sticking, you know the quality is good. You should also check that the zipper on a garment is well stitched. Please remember that garments are made by humans and while they are quality checked only a percentage of production will be checked. You want to make sure that your zipper does not catch in the stitching as you open and close it; occasionally it will and this is just down to human error. If the zipper sticks, just ask for a different item.

18. Ask questions

Let brands know that you are paying attention, it helps them to give you what you want. Don't be afraid to ask where garments are made, etc. If you don't like something that they are doing, tell them, but do not stop shopping with them. Give them the opportunity to improve. Don't let perfect be the enemy of great.

19. Show loyalty

It goes without saying that when you find a brand you love, you will keep going back. You will know their fit, which makes it easier for you to shop online. Increasingly, stores and brands are introducing loyalty schemes which reward their most loyal customers, so there are added little bonuses along the way.

20. Stay focused

Stay focused on your personal style. While you shouldn't take it as gospel, keep your shopping list on your phone. Use it as a reminder of the pieces that you are missing to pull your looks together and give them a bit of attitude. That is not to say that you should close your mind to things that are not on your list, as that will result in you missing out on some great finds. While you will initially have to train yourself to stay focused, as you practise everything that you have learned in the book, this will be something you don't have to think about. Over time, you will get better at spotting those fab pieces that just work for your style.

CHAPTER 27

Top Garment Care Tips

Do you know anybody who enjoys laundry? Washing, ironing, matching socks? Life is just too short for all of this. So, over the years, as a busy mother myself who would rather do anything than spend her time doing laundry, I thought about how I could simplify and spend less time on these chores, making more time for doing the things I love.

As well as saving you time, the following tips can also help you to prolong the life of your clothes, reduce your utility bills and help you to make real contributions towards sustainability.

Before I get stuck in, I have to stress that you should never deviate from care label instructions. These have been carefully researched and tested by the manufacturer. Fabric comes with recommendations from the fabric mills. Then the brand's design teams will always make further recommendations based on factors like keeping the shape of the garment and details intact, the lifetime value of the garment and the trims that have been used. To deviate from these instructions is risky, especially if you love or have invested in the item.

With that said, here are my top tips for caring for your garments.

1. Washing

Did you know that most clothes only need a very short wash. You will use less water and less electricity. The biggest bonus is you can get all of your washing done in about half the time, so a morning of doing jobs around the house will allow you to get through several wash cycles clearing the whole family's washing in one swoop. I can empty all of the washing baskets in a house of 4 adults (with a gym-bunny daughter and 2 sons who are obviously out to impress!) in a morning. There is a huge sense of achievement, as I whizz through it all feeling like a washing superhero. Then I ignore the build-up in between, from one weekend to the next.

Washing black

When it comes to your own clothes, I have found that if I wash all my blacks together they stay pristine for longer. This means nothing else gets into the wash with them. Other dark items like jeans, towels, etc can rub on the surface of more delicate fabrics, giving them a worn look before their time. I observe these rules strictly and nobody else is allowed to wash my clothes. I have black leggings that are 8 years old and still look as good as new.

Washing white

As with blacks, whites should also be washed strictly on their own. I always wash my own whites separate to the family washing. It just helps to keep them looking newer for longer. At the very least, make sure that your white fabrics do not get washed with towels which will rub on the surface and can cause pilling. Every few washes, use a small scoop of Napisan with your detergent for an extra whitening boost.

Washing creams

Cream items should always be treated as delicates. In a lot of fabrics, cream is a colour that is very hard to dye and colour fastness cannot be guaranteed. Always wash cream items in a non-biological detergent on the shortest wash.

2. Detergents

Invest in good washing detergents. These are actually more important in the removal of stains than long washing cycles. I would advise having a selection of different detergents for different tasks:

- For coloured garments, use non-biological detergents to protect the colours.
- For whites, use detergents with optical whiteners.
- For your woollens and delicates, only use a hand wash soap detergent.
- For blacks, you can get special detergents that have been specially formulated to keep your blacks black.

3. Drying

The best way to dry your clothes, where possible, is always going to be on a clothesline. Tumble drying is hard on electricity and hard on your clothes. In fact, on a lot of the care labels on the clothes I design, I say no tumble drying at all.

A great way to ensure there is as little creasing as possible is to dry your clothes on hangers. This cuts down on the amount of handing and allows creases to fall out when drying. If you want to soften any completely dry items, pop them in the dryer on a cold cycle for 4/5 minutes which will fluff them up nicely.

4. Ditch the iron

There are very few things in your wardrobe that actually need to be ironed. The things you should absolutely not be spending your life ironing are underwear, socks, sports gear, and anything that stretches and is a close fit to the body, as your body heat will remove any wrinkles within a few minutes. Of course, there will be things that you might have heart failure if I suggested not ironing them, say shirts, for example. But these would really be my only exception. If you have dried clothes as recommended above, you will see how little creasing needs to be dealt with. If you line dry clothes, don't throw them all in a basket as you will be adding to the creases. Instead, hang them straight away.

5. Steaming

This is one of my favourite tips. When I first suggested this to our team, I was met with some resistance, but everybody quickly came around to the idea and are now diehard steamer fans. While we are not fans of ironing, we are also not fans of creasing in general. Get yourself a valet steamer, it will change your life. It is one of those upright steamers with a coat hanger and decent-sized water tank attached. When it comes to my white shirts, which are my everyday uniform, I will have up to 10 garments hanging on this and will whizz through steaming them in about 15 minutes. Also, all my jersey pieces get a little steam as they are going into my wardrobe. Steaming adds to the softness of the fabric. It is also a great way to freshen items in-between wears. I can get a few days out of our loose-fitting white shirts by steaming them in-between wears. Your steamers can also be used on curtains and can even freshen your bedsheets in-between washes!

6. Freshen

You do not need to wash clothes every time you wear them. Here are a few ways to freshen garments up in-between wears.

- Hang the garment on a hanger, on a clothesline, for an hour. This is great for removing odours.
- If an item can be tumble dried, pop it in the dryer for 15 minutes with a damp washcloth.
- Steam kills bacteria and is a great way to freshen up items that are worn close to the skin but not dirty or stained. Use your steamer. Pop a couple of drops of your favourite scent in the water. Don't use oil-based scents as these may damage your steamer, but perfumes are perfect.

7. Woollens & cashmeres

Only use mild hand wash liquids and never powders, these are kinder to delicates. Do not be tempted to put woollens in the machine if the care label says hand wash only (even using a hand wash setting)! You might get away with it, but it is at your own risk and you are potentially shortening the life of your garment. Like all of your other pieces, woollens only need occasional laundering. Freshen them up as above in-between.

Hand wash the garment in lukewarm water. Never use hot water as this can cause shrinkage. Squeeze the garment, gently. Never rub as this will cause pilling. Never wring as this stretches the garment. Rinse and then give a final rinse in your favourite fabric conditioner. Squeeze out as much water as possible. At this point, I would always give heavier items a short spin in the washing machine, but I would do them individually so that they do not rub against each other. Lay each piece on a large towel and reshape it without stretching. Then roll up the towel and leave it laid flat in a place where the air can circulate. I have a couple of drying racks mounted on a wall, close to the ceiling in my utility room which are perfect for this purpose. When completely dry, each piece gets popped into the dryer with a scented dryer sheet on a cold cycle for no more than 3/4 minutes to fluff them up nicely. While this might seem quite time-consuming, it's not really when you do a few pieces together. Fluffing or pilling is normal in garments with a high natural content. You will definitely see it on knitted items which are 100% cashmere or wool. If they do not pill, they have been mixed with another fibre to prevent it. In-between wears, use a battery-operated pill remover to get rid of any fluff that has gathered on the surface.

8. Hangers

I cannot stress enough the importance of using good hangers. Get rid of the cheap plastic slippery hangers as they will drive you nuts when everything falls off them. They also do nothing to inspire you when you are looking into your wardrobe. Invest in good hangers that all match. When you open your wardrobe and everything is uniform, it sub-consciously has a calming effect. It will also make you feel better about everything in your wardrobe. You will be more inclined to keep it looking great and when it is done well, it prevents you from putting anything in there that won't work with everything else! You will need 3 types: coat hangers which are the wide ones, shirt hangers which are narrower and trousers/skirt hangers which can either have clips or a bar for hanging things over.

9. Shoulder covers

These are great for popping over your jackets and coats when they are not in use. They keep dust off and

Steam kills bacteria and is a great way to freshen up items that are worn close to the skin but not dirty or stained. Use your steamer.

make these pieces feel more loved, which is good for your head.

10. De-bobblers

These come in a few different types. They can be sweater combs or battery-operated shaver-like devices. They are used for removing the balls that form on the surface of your woollens and knitwear. I recommend that you only use the battery-operated version on delicates. The combs are fine on tightly woven fabrics, and knits, but should never be used on delicates or lace items.

11. Leathers and suedes

Never ever wash these. They should only be cleaned by leather specialists.

12. Sequins, Velcro and jewellery

We all love them, but they can spell disaster around delicate fabrics and items, so keep them well away. Store anything with sequins inside out in your wardrobe. Be very careful of the jewellery that you wear with delicate fabrics. Rough edges and claws can destroy delicate items and cause wear and tear on the front of garments.

13. Travelling

As with storing delicates, use tissue paper to fold your delicate items when you travel. Another little tip... when shops receive hanging stock, it comes covered in plastic garment bags. Shops are always looking for ways to be more sustainable, so they will be delighted to give them to you if you ask. They are very useful for wrapping your favourite pieces when you are travelling, preventing creasing.

14. Have an emergency kit

Always have an emergency kit in your bag. Things like small pins for when you lose a button, baby wipes for unexpected spills, a needle and thread for a hem that gets pulled down, and scissors for stray threads. These will ensure that your outfit is always immaculate.

15. Clothes brushes and sticky rollers

If you wear a lot of black, it is very stressful when you are going into a meeting to discover that fluff has stuck to you, the dog has rubbed up against you or your favourite sweater has shed all over your black jeans. I never go anywhere without a sticky roller in my bag. Also, keep a clothes brush in your wardrobe and brush down your jackets and coats at the end of the day so that you are not bringing outside dust into your wardrobe.

16. Spot cleaning and baby wipes

Another essential in your handbag is a packet of baby wipes (the biodegradable ones of course!). They are handy for spot cleaning your clothes and even your shoes!

17. Storing your out of season clothes

Store your winter clothes during summer and your summer clothes during winter. There are several benefits to doing this. You will create more space for the clothes that you are actually going to be wearing. You will be able to see exactly what you have. You will be protecting the out of season pieces from dust and getting grubby and worn looking from being squashed in with and rubbed against other garments.

My out of season clothes always go into the attic. If you don't have an attic, at least try to store them out of your sight. Put everything away in strong plastic boxes. Remember, wrap everything like a future present to yourself so that you will be excited every year when you unpack the boxes.

18. Storing coats

Coats do not need to be cleaned often, but it is a good time to give them a once a year freshen up just before you store them. Store them in suit bags, preferably in another place where you won't see them at all during the summer, so you will have the added benefit of loving them all over again when you unpack them the following autumn.

19. Storing delicates

We include white items as delicates. Always make sure garments are freshly laundered and steamed. You might wonder why would you bother steaming something that you are just going to fold up and put into storage? This has less to do with the storing and more to do with how you feel about unpacking the piece the following winter/ summer. Like the coats, it makes you fall in love with the pieces all over again. You could go one step further and wrap them in tissue paper and a Ziplock bag. Save any tissue paper that comes with your purchases for this purpose.

20. Storing cashmere and woollens

The biggest nightmare when unpacking your woollens after months in storage is finding that they have been damaged by moths. The good news is, in 25 years of running my business, I have yet to have anything ruined in storage by moths, so it doesn't happen all that often, but you can be unlucky. A stray one can find its way into your wardrobe and hibernate in your cosy woollens. I won't go into the skin-crawling details, but the damage is done not by the moths sitting eating your woollens in the wardrobe, but by the baby moths hatching. So, we want to make sure that your woollens are freshly laundered, stored completely dry and aired. Traditionally, mothballs would be used, but these do not smell the best. Cedar balls or lavender are equally effective and smell much nicer. Lavender is easy to grow, so have a bush or two in your garden and harvest your own lavender at the end of the summer. This can be stored in little pouches stored in your folded wools. A little spray of lavender can give an extra layer of protection.

Section 7 Summary

I hope you have picked up lots of tips and hacks in this section. Let us know how you get on with them. If you have any to add yourself, we would love to know about them. You can use the #empoweredbystyle hashtag on Instagram and we will pick up on them and share them with our followers crediting you for them.

Use the tips in this section to save yourself 10 minutes here, 20 minutes there. Keep a running total for a few weeks and see how much time you can save yourself on fruitless shopping trips, unnecessary laundry chores and second-guessing yourself.

You saved that time, it is yours. What are you going to do with it?

Maybe a spa trip with a friend who has saved her time as well?

Maybe you will take up a new hobby?

Maybe you will learn something new to inspire you even further?

Or maybe you will just chill out a bit more and enjoy a few minutes here and there so that you are happy and more present in your life.

CHAPTER 28

The Empowered Style Goddess

Now that we have taken this journey together, I hope that you can look back and see how you have evolved from the start.

I hope that you will have:

- Noted where predictable curveballs can occur so that they don't come at you out of the blue.
- Eliminated any of the 7 mistakes that you recognise when shopping.
- Learned that what you wear matters and will have a plan for how you want to show up so you can achieve your big goals.
- Understood the importance of Evolving your style.

- Picked up some tips on responsible consumption so that you can effortlessly develop a sustainable wardrobe.
- Established your style type.
- Established your body shape.
- Learned how to use colour in your wardrobe.
- Discovered all of the various wardrobe types and which ones you will use to build and evolve your own.
- Become aware of the lies we tell ourselves that do not serve us well.
- Learned how to develop and keep evolving your style.
- Learned how and when to Assess, Evolve and Refresh your wardrobe.
- Benefited from our complete reference section of tips for styling, shopping and garment care.

This book has literally squeezed every word out of my head. I expected to have it written in 3 months, but it took me over a year. Every spare minute at the weekends and in the evenings after work, I was working at it. Every time I stepped away, my thinking evolved, the structure changed, or new chapters were added.

While I was doing it, my own wardrobe took a serious hit. I didn't get to do my Assess | Evolve | Refresh process when I normally would, resulting in me feeling like I was on the back foot. And as for the washing and housework, well that was totally out of control.

It got me thinking that it's all fine and well having the big plan, but what happens when life takes over and it all goes tits up? What happens then and how do you stop it all descending into chaos?

For me, a successful work week looks like this. I get up at 5am, I do 20 minutes of exercise, 20 minutes of journaling and 20 minutes of learning. This is followed by a breakfast smoothie and an hour and a half undisturbed, working on the most important things I need to do for my business. Yes, I do have kids in college and they do live at home. Because we live in the country, it means that I'm still dropping and collecting, so by 7am my day has probably already been hijacked by lifts to buses and train runs. My 20 minutes exercise and 20 minutes learning often happen at the same time. My gratitude journaling is done on the nearest scrap of paper to the boiling kettle, and all too often I drag myself out of the bed already running late.

However, even on the mornings that it all goes south, I refuse to give up a few things that can help rescue the day. Even if I feel like dragging on the things I stepped out of the day before, I will hit the shower and practise my gratitude while I'm in there. I will put on something that reflects the day I am planning. Even if it is a day in the design room, which means that nobody will see me, I will still dress for me. I will still, at the least, do my eyebrows and pop on some mascara and some of my favourite perfume. Every day will be improved just by doing that.

None of these things take any more time and make a world of difference to my mindset and personal sense of worth.

When the washing piles high, I will smile and close the door on it and try to pop on a load here and there amid the chaos. As long as nobody is going out the door naked, I'll take that as a win.

If I don't get everything done that I planned in the day, I will just put it on my list for the next day and refuse to think about it for the rest of the evening. I will email myself if I think of something work-related and when my daughter and I (she works with me at the time of writing this) find ourselves talking shop in the evenings, one of us will say "pineapple" and we immediately stop.

Whatever your life looks like, it is life-changing when you make the first hour or even half-hour in the day yours.

When you are caring for others, especially young families, I know it's easier said than done but try to get up half an hour earlier than them, so that you feel satisfied before the chaos of the day even begins. If this is just too hard, take that half-hour at night to pamper yourself. Light a scented candle, turn on some relaxing music and take off your makeup. Then leave ready your outfit for the following morning so you can just jump up and get dressed in five minutes and go.

The steps that you take to create a wardrobe that is focused will create, by default, a more focused mind. What you wear affects your mindset, it affects how you show up and perform. It is the first step in attracting what you want to show up in your life. When you adopt and lean into this thinking, it is simple, but it is also life-changing.

Lurking beneath the surface in every woman is a goddess. Wake her up, let her come out to play. She is the soul mate who goes everywhere with you. She is your best friend, your first and your last love. You were born with her and you will die with her. You don't need anyone else's validation.

And remember… you are a goddess if you say you are!

Lurking beneath the surface in every woman is a goddess. Wake her up, let her come out to play. She is the soul mate who goes everywhere with you. She is your best friend, your first and your last love. You were born with her and you will die with her. You don't need anyone else's validation.

Book Extras

Empowered by Style Wardrobe Challenge

From time to time we will be running wardrobe challenges. If you would like to take part, pop over to our website here and sign up to be the first to hear when the doors open.

https://marygrant.com/wardrobe-challenge/

In the meantime, here's a little personal challenge for you!

Until it becomes second nature, challenge yourself on everything that you are tempted to buy. If it doesn't tick at least one of these boxes, step away!

- Will I be able to sleep tonight if I don't buy it?
- Will I use it at least once every two weeks?
- Does it fit into my lifestyle?
- Does it work with at least two other things in my wardrobe?
- Does it take me in a new direction?

Acknowledgements

A huge thank you to my family, Nora Grant (Mum) and Mick Grant (Dad), my kids Bronagh, Conor & James, who sometimes just stand and look at me like I have two heads when there are hair-brained ideas spurting out of me. Thank you for not locking me up (yet).

To my team in Bronagh Galvin, Breda Ryan, Andrea Hamilton, Fiona Hagan, Dee Hagan, Pat McCartan, Lisa Matthews, Siobhan Rooney and Helen Martin, who gave me tremendous support while I was writing this, and who work tirelessly every day to help our customers feel amazing. You are the heroes.

To our loyal customers, many who have been with us since the very beginning, I appreciate you and everything that I have learned from you. I look forward to serving you for another 25 years.

To Dent Global and especially Daniel Priestly who changed my life the day he said, "You are standing on a mountain of value." To my accountability buddies, Paul

McGillivray, Jeannie McGillivray, Sonja Leeson, Jane Malyon, Lorraine Gannon, Vicki Wusche, Jonathan Farrar Areej Khataybih and Obi James, who have been there every step of the way. Thank you for never rolling your eyes while I'm figuring out my next steps!

To my beta readers who gave me such great feedback and helped me to make this book better than it ever could have been without them. Adeline Molloy, Andrea Hamilton, Dee Hagan, Obi James, Barbara Katthri, Lucy Barkas and Bronagh Galvin.

To Leila Green and the team at Known Publishing. Thank you for the tireless work that you do with non-authors like me who write books for their businesses. I am sure we give you brain damage every day. Thank you also to Lucy McCarraher who put me on the path to writing a book when I was clueless and Alison Jones whose 10-day book challenge sharpened my thinking.

Thank you to all the people who helped me to build a brand that has survived for over 25 years. Shelly Corkery, Nikki Creedon, Louise Flanagan, Kate O'Dwyer, Jenny Turner, Bernie Flanagan who all helped me to fine tune my early collections with their invaluable feedback. Also to all the members of the press who supported me over the years, especially Constance Harris, Deirdre McQuillan and Barbara Power who supported every single collection even if they sometimes lovingly questioned where it was all going. I am eternally grateful to you all.

Finally, a special mention to my good friend Johnny. Without our 10,000+ emails, spouting pure rubbish, I never would have realised I had enough words in me to take on the task of writing a whole book. You raised me up with your encouragement to just be an unedited version of myself. I hope I have passed a bit of that on to everyone who reads this book.

Printed in Great Britain
by Amazon

66693741R00208